STAR WARS®

Power of the Empire

Dalmatian Press, LLC, 2005. All rights reserved. Printed in the U.S.A.
The DALMATIAN PRESS name, logo, Tear and Share, and spotted spine are trademarks of Dalmatian Press, LLC,
Franklin, Tennessee 37067. No part of this book may be reproduced or copied in any form without the written
permission from the copyright owner.

05 06 07 08 CLI 10 9 8 7 6
13888: STAR WARS - POWER OF THE EMPIRE

The Death Star

HOW MANY TIE FIGHTERS ARE IN THIS SQUADRON?

Your answer: _____

Answer: 12

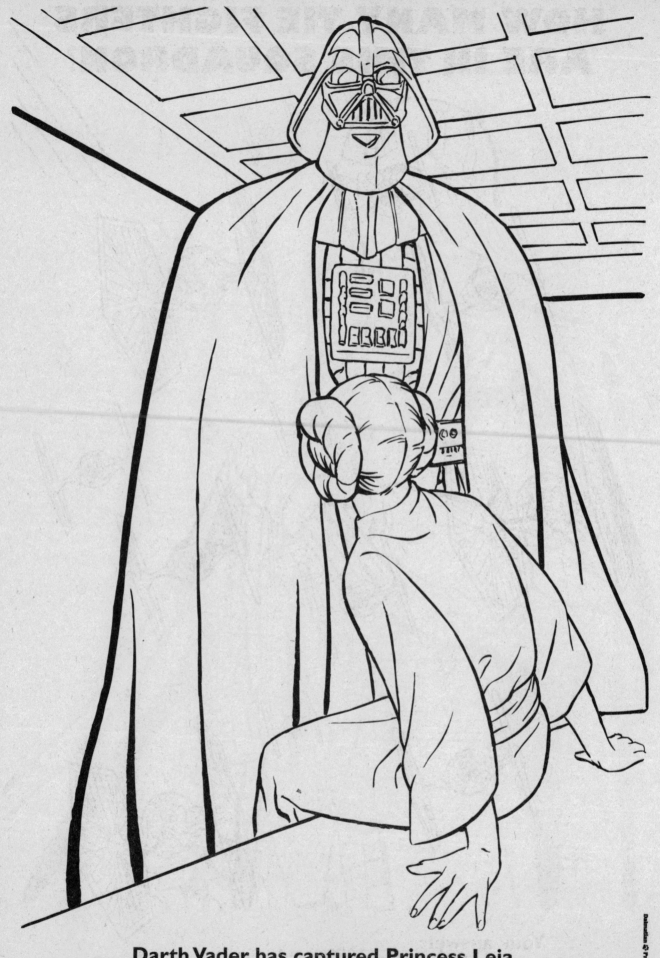

Darth Vader has captured Princess Leia.

Darth Vader ignites his lightsaber.

How many different words can you make from

THE DEATH STAR?

_____   _____

_____   _____

_____   _____

_____   _____

_____   _____

_____   _____

_____   _____

_____   _____

What kind of space ships are these?

A. X-WING FIGHTERS

B. TIE FIGHTERS

C. STAR DESTROYERS

Answer: B

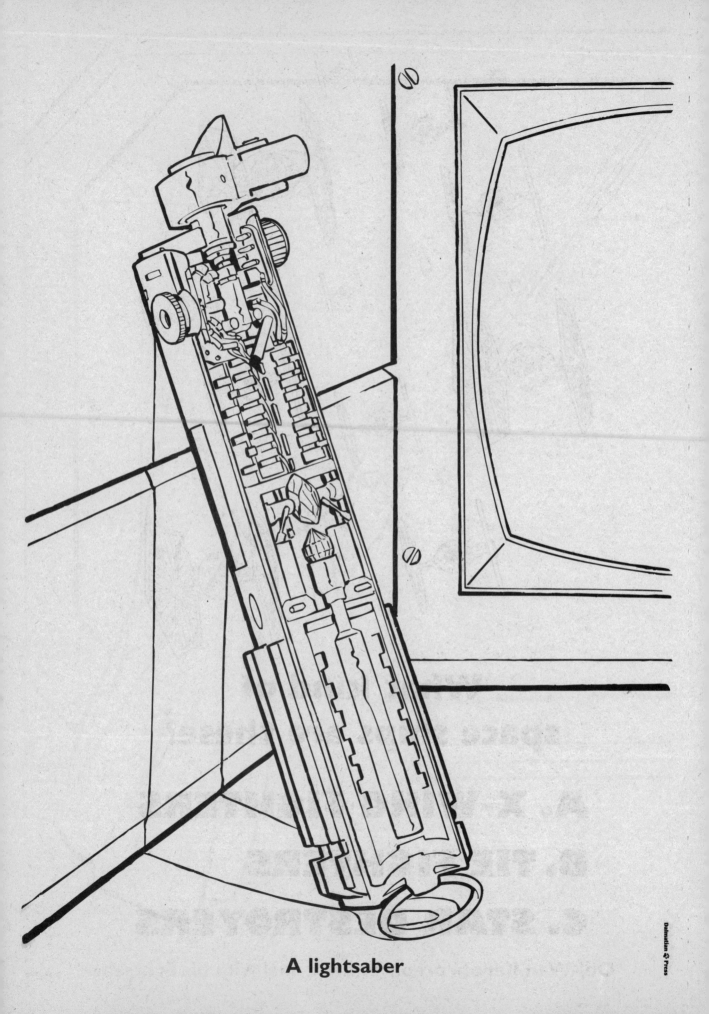

A lightsaber

Obi-Wan Kenobi prepares for a duel with his lightsaber.

Emperor Palpatine is Darth Vader's Master.

The Sith hate the Jedi.

Yoda is a Jedi Master.

He has trained many generations of Jedi.

USE THE GRID BELOW TO DRAW
YODA
ON THE OPPOSITE PAGE.

**Luke has crashed his X-wing
on Dagobah, where Yoda lives.**

Yoda lifts Luke's X-wing out of the mud, so Luke can help his friends.

HELP LUKE FIND HIS WAY THROUGH THE MAZE

Lead Luke back to his X-wing to save his friends.

How many different words can you make from

DAGOBAH SYSTEM?

_____   _____

_____   _____

_____   _____

_____   _____

_____   _____

_____   _____

_____   _____

_____   _____

Yoda trains Luke to be a Jedi.

Training to be a Jedi is hard work.

JEDI TRAINING CROSSWORD PUZZLE

Down:

1. Yoda lives on the _____ system.
3. Yoda has long pointy _____ on the sides of his head.

Across:

2. Luke sees _____ in the cave.
4. _____ is a great Jedi Master.
5. On the Dagobah system there are many _____ and other creepy crawly life-forms.

Dalmatian Press

WHICH YODA IS DIFFERENT?

Answer: D

**Luke goes into a cave and
sees something that frightens him...**

It's Darth Vader!

HOW ARE DARTH VADER AND LUKE SKYWALKER RELATED?

A. FATHER AND SON

B. UNCLE AND NEPHEW

C. MOTHER AND DAUGHTER

D. SECOND COUSINS

Dalmatian Press

DRAW THE OTHER HALF OF DARTH VADER'S HELMET.

Darth Vader and Luke Skywalker duel with their lightsabers.

Luke duels valiantly.

USE THE GRID BELOW TO DRAW
EMPEROR PALPATINE
ON THE OPPOSITE PAGE.

CAN YOU ESCAPE
THE DEATH STAR MAZE...

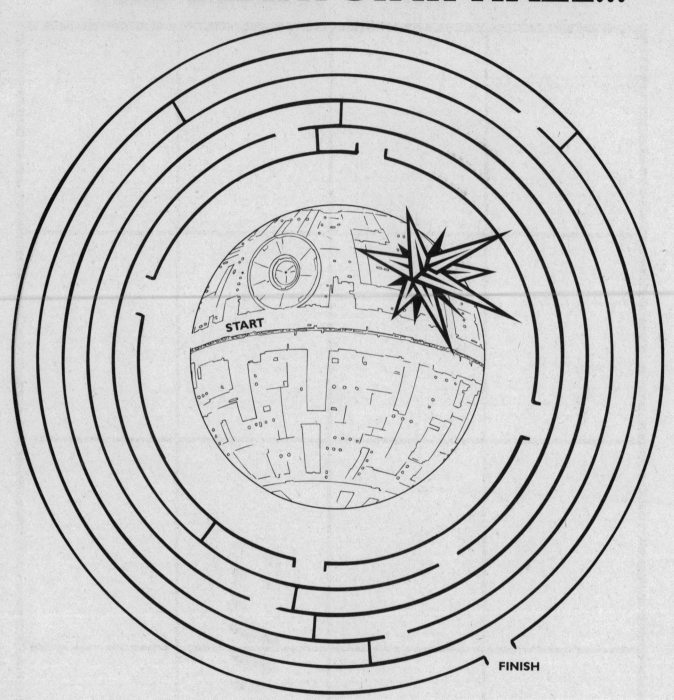

START

FINISH

BEFORE IT EXPLODES?

Obi-Wan Kenobi

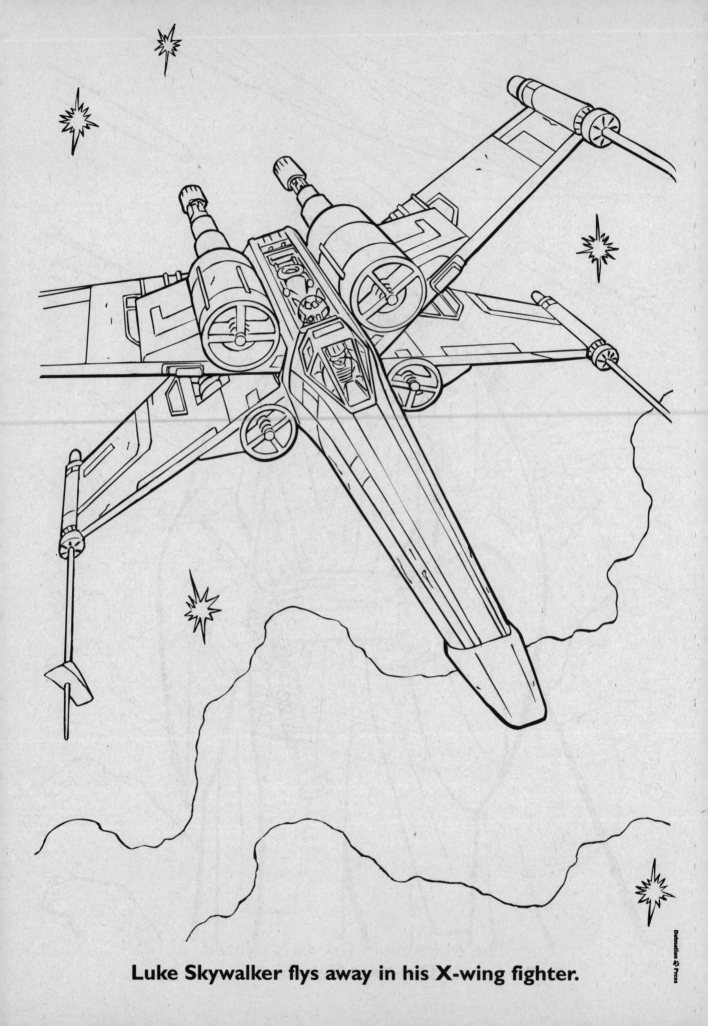

Luke Skywalker flys away in his X-wing fighter.

**The *Millennium Falcon* is piloted
by Han Solo and his Wookiee, Chewbacca.**

PILOT THE MILLENNIUM FALCON SAFELY THROUGH THE ASTEROID FIELD.

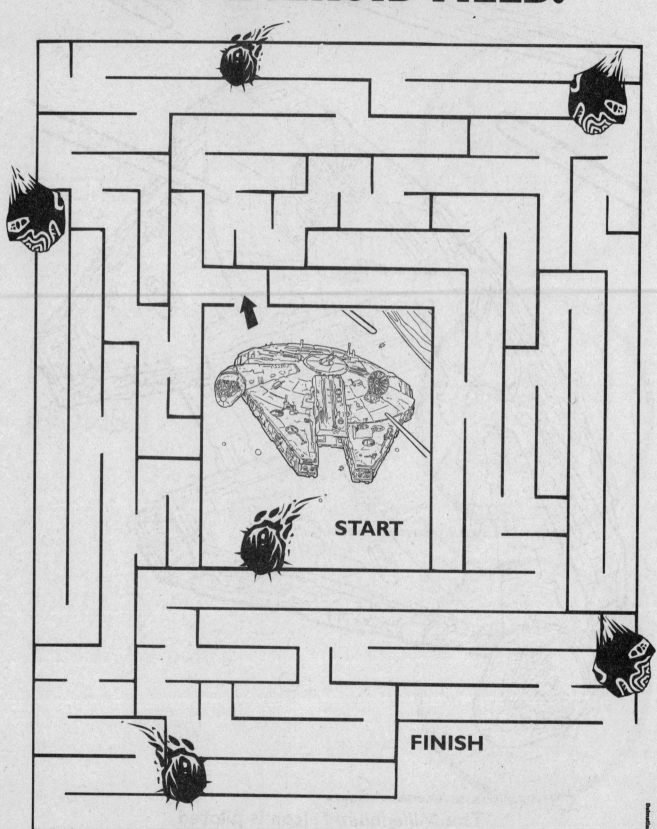

START

FINISH

MATCH EACH PICTURE TO THE CORRECT CHARACTER NAME.

1 ____

3 ____

A. DARTH VADER

B. OBI-WAN KENOBI

C. LUKE SKYWALKER

Han and Chewbacca blast their way out of trouble.

WOOKIEE WORD SEARCH

Look forwards, backwards, across, down and diagonally to find the words listed below:

Han Solo
Cross-bow
Cloud City

Blaster
Carbonite

Chewbacca
Falcon
Chewie

C	A	R	B	O	N	I	T	E
L	H	A	N	S	O	L	O	F
O	C	E	I	W	E	H	C	A
U	R	Q	W	O	O	K	I	L
D	O	A	Z	B	Z	F	C	C
C	S	L	A	S	A	A	N	O
I	S	B	O	W	A	C	E	N
T	W	H	T	K	I	E	C	A
Y	R	E	T	S	A	L	B	A

"I see two banthas down there
but I don't see any Sand People."

BANTHA TRACKS

Can you lead the banthas through the desert maze?

START

FINISH

The Rebels have won a great battle.

They reward their heroes with medals.

An astromech droid

Droids make great friends.

R2-D2 and C-3PO have had many adventures.

There are many different kinds of astromech droids. Color the two that are the same.

A

B

C

D

Answer: A and D

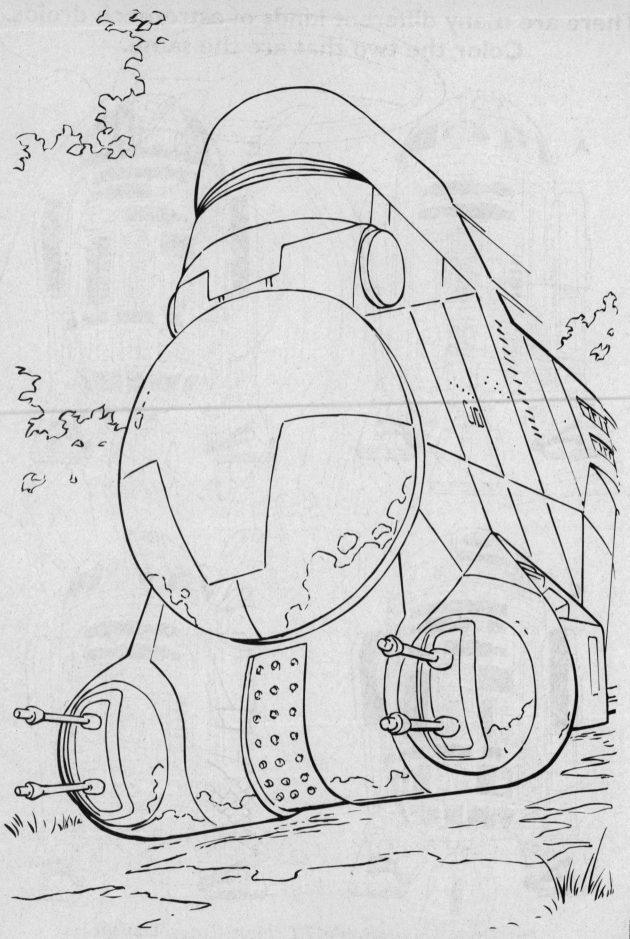

Battle droids use special vehicles for transport.

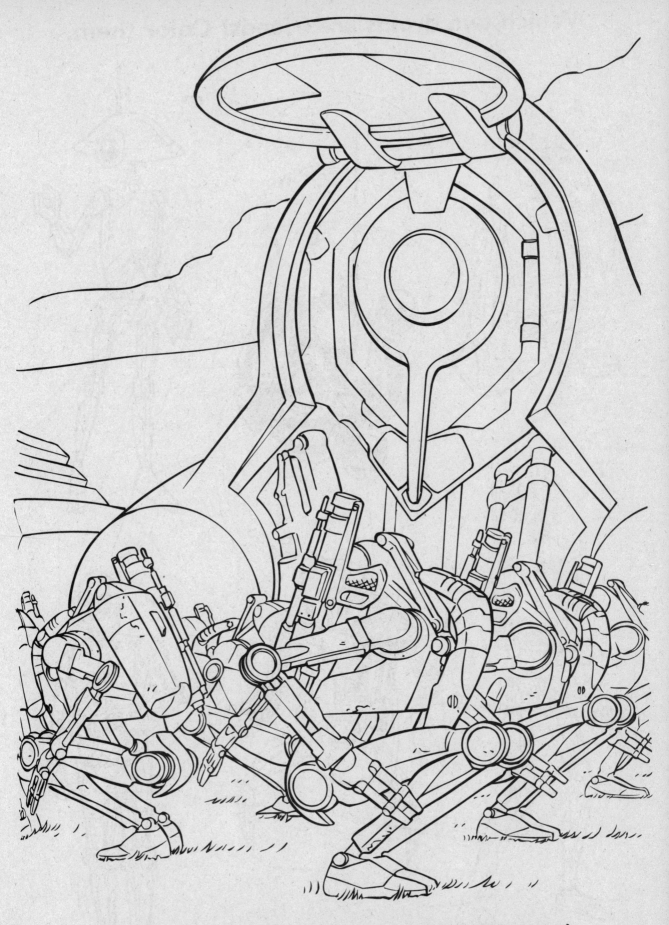

The Trade Federation MTT (Multi-Troop Transport) opens, and the battle droids unfold to get ready for battle.

Which two droids are friends? Color them.

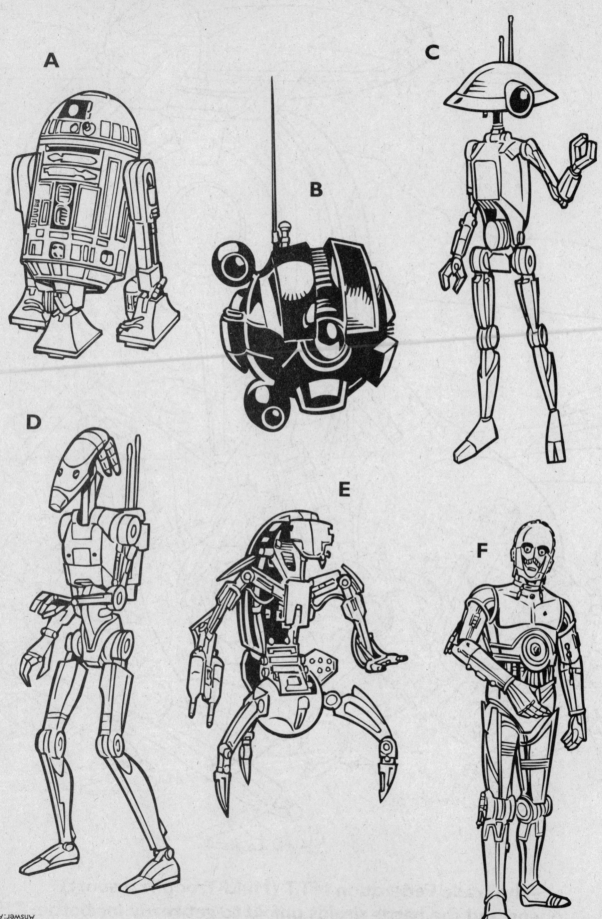

A

B

C

D

E

F

Dalmatian Press

Some droids are dangerous.

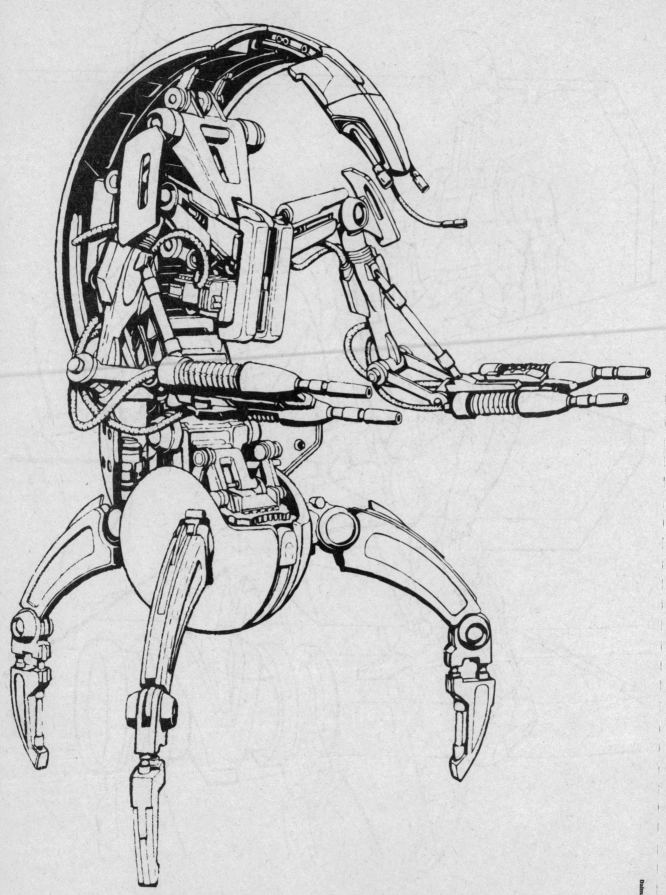

Destroyer droids have laser cannons.

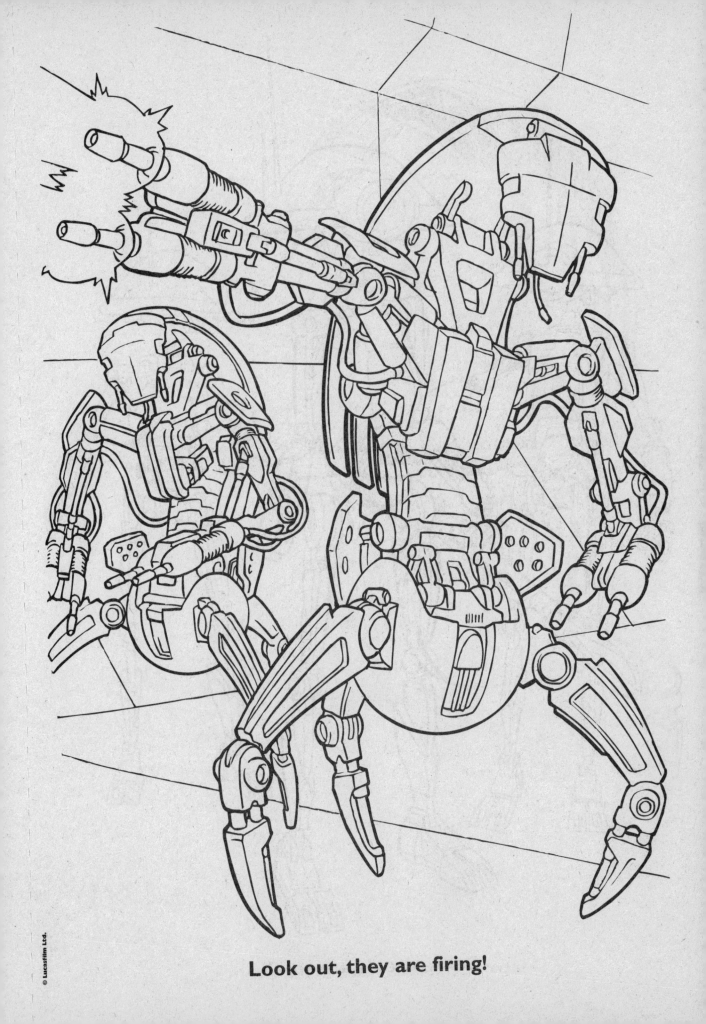

Look out, they are firing!

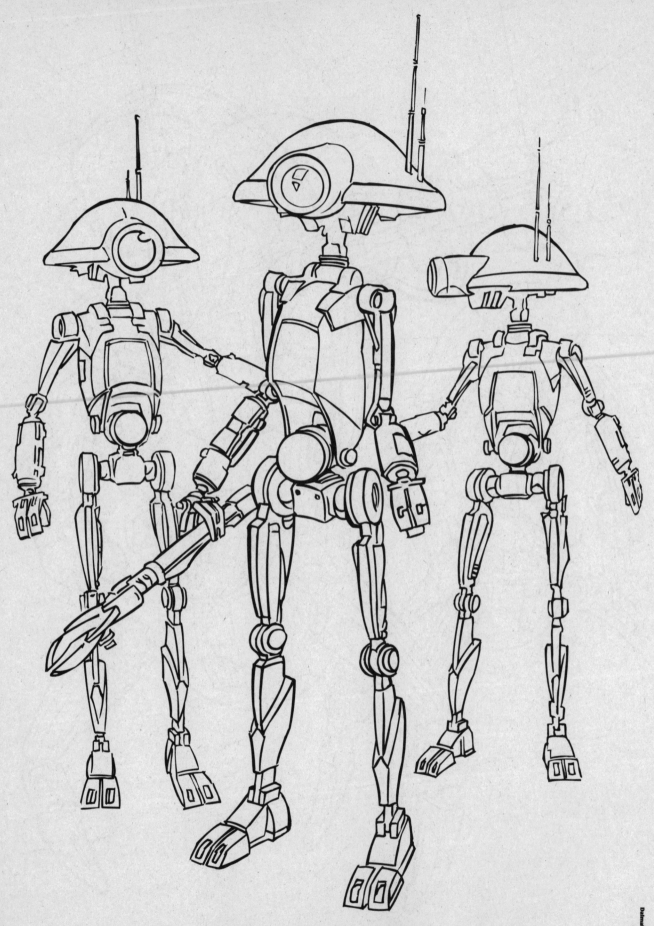

Some droids are small.

Dalmatian Press

Some droids are no bigger than a ball.

Battle droids have captured Queen Amidala of Naboo.

Maybe R2-D2 and his friends can help.

Which three battle droids are different?

Connect the dots to see what kind of droid helps prepare for the Boonta Eve Podrace.

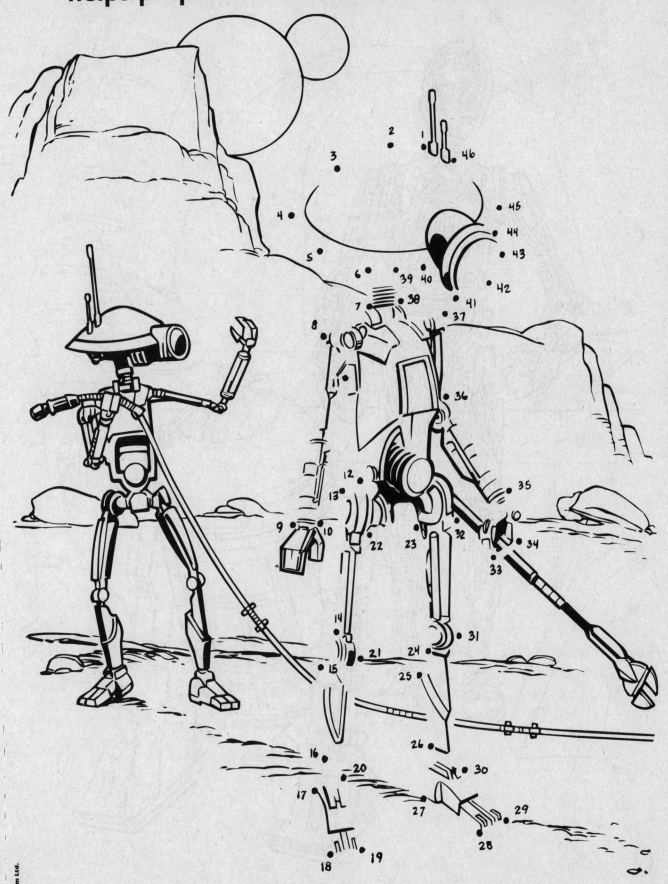

Answer: A pit droid

C-3PO meets R2-D2.

R2-D2 repairs a Podracer.

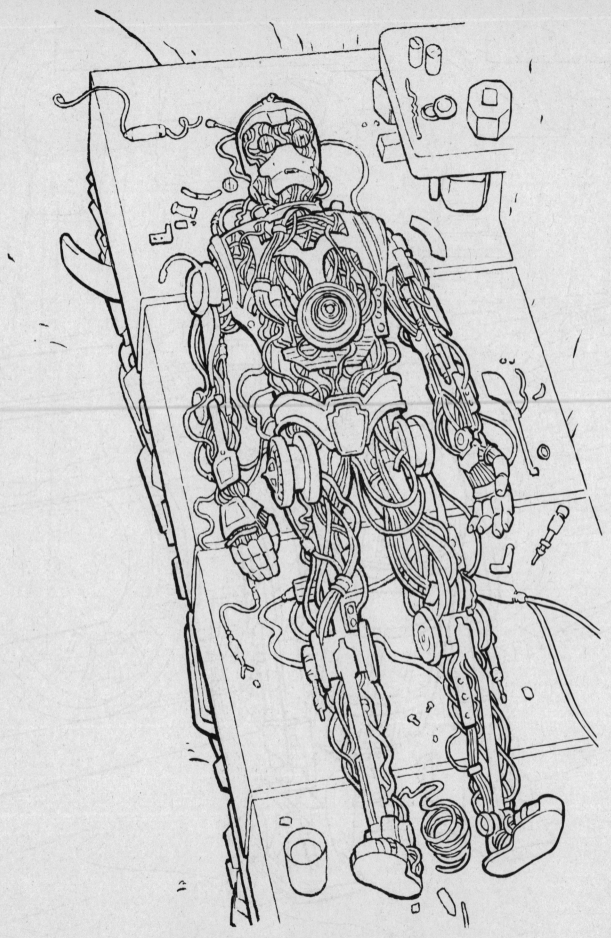

C-3PO is not quite finished yet.

TC-14 brings the waiting Jedi some refreshment.

DROID SCANS

What droid is shown on the scan below?

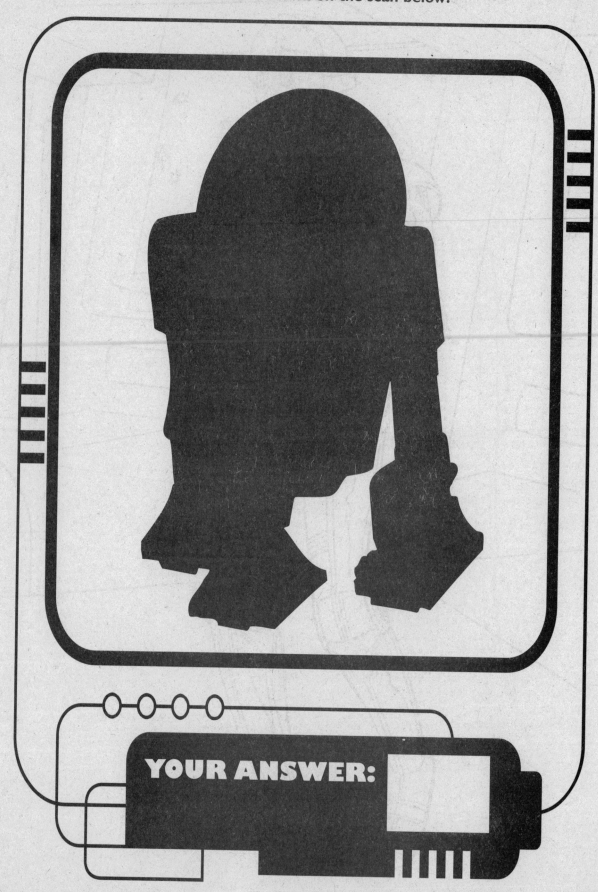

YOUR ANSWER:

Answer: R2-D2 (or possibly any astromech droid with a round dome)

DROID DRAWINGS

Complete the rest of R2-D2's body with your own drawing

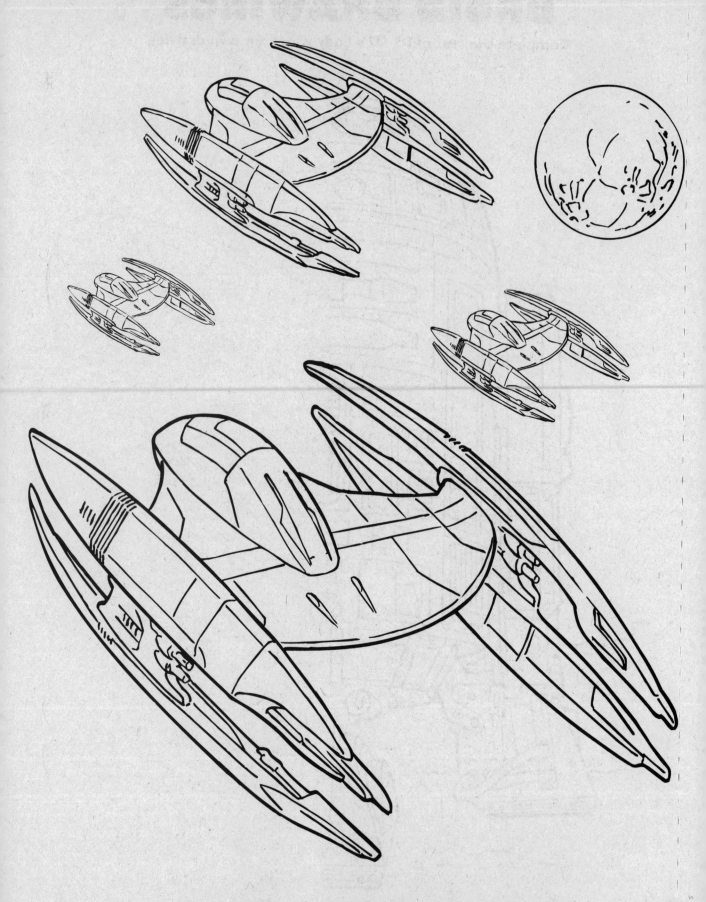

**Droid fighters can fly through space
and look like space ships.**

A Trade Federation Battleship

Anakin and R2-D2 join the battle in a Naboo Starfighter.

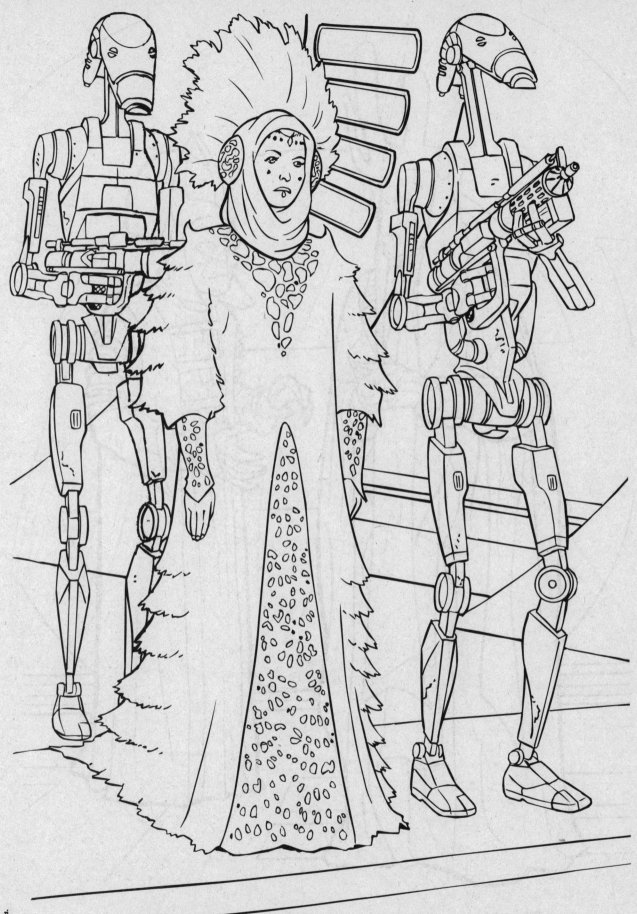

The queen has been captured!

**The Neimoidians from the Trade Federation
are greedy and cowardly.**

**Connect the dots to see whom Nute Gunray
and Rune Haako are so afraid of.**

Answer: Darth Sidious

Rune Haako

Nute Gunray

Darth Maul is a Sith apprentice...

...to his master Darth Sidious, a Sith Lord.

The Jedi will help protect Naboo...

...from the battle droids.

Darth Sidious sends Darth Maul on a mission...

...to capture the escaped Queen Amidala of Naboo.

Darth Maul sends out probe droids to find the queen.

Qui-Gon Jinn will stop them.

Queen Amidala of Naboo

HELP THE QUEEN LAND
HER SPACE CRUISER ON THE PLANET BELOW.

START

FINISH

FINISH DRAWING THE QUEEN

Complete the rest of Queen Amidala's body with your own drawing.

**The deflector shields on
the Queen's ship help keep her safe.**

**Anakin runs from Darth Maul
while Qui-Gon Jinn prepares to protect him.**

Darth Maul pursues them on his Sith speeder.

Qui-Gon Jinn protects Anakin from attack.

**Darth Maul is a skilled fighter, trained
to use the dark side of the Force.**

**Qui-Gon and Obi-Wan wait to begin
negotiations with the Trade Federation.**

"I've got a bad feeling about this...."

Qui-Gon Jinn is a noble Jedi Master.

Qui-Gon's apprentice is Obi-Wan Kenobi.

Padmé meets Anakin for the first time.

The Force is strong with Anakin Skywalker.

Qui-Gon Jinn defends himself...

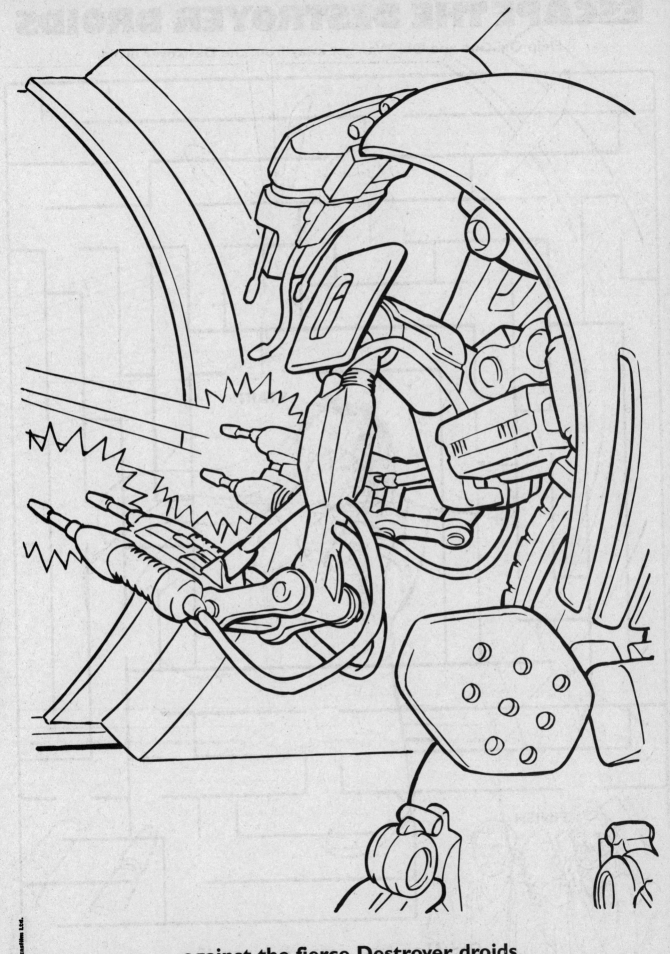

...against the fierce Destroyer droids.

ESCAPE THE DESTROYER DROIDS

Help Qui-Gon and Obi-Wan get away from the Destroyer droid.

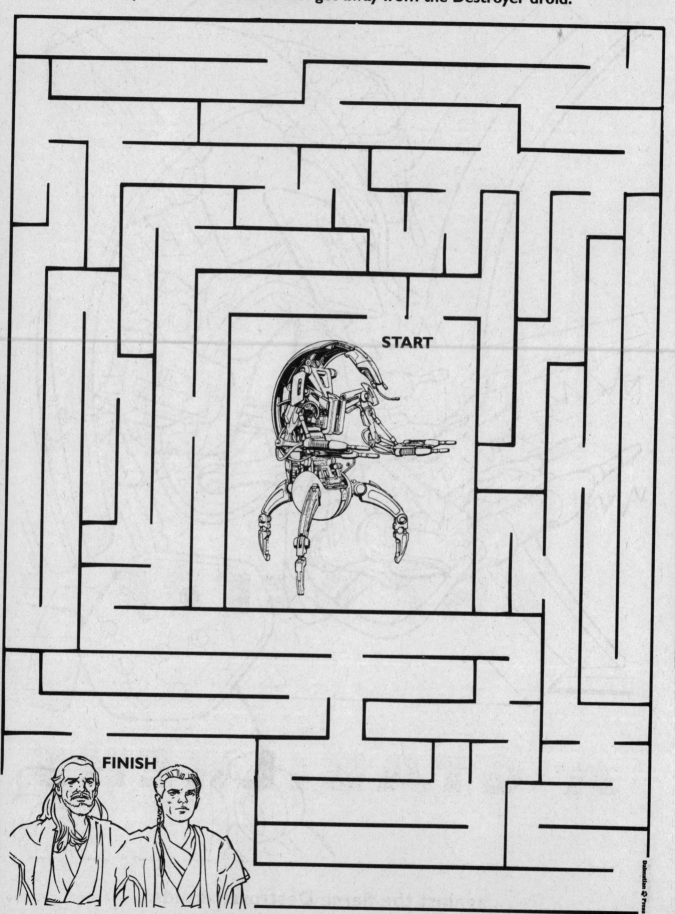

START

FINISH

JEDI WORD SCRAMBLE

Unscramble the words below to see what Obi-Wan's two greatest weapons are.

EHT OCFRE

- - -   - - - - -

A GTABILREHS

- - - - - - - - - -

Answer: The Force and A Lightsaber

Obi-Wan Kenobi also defends himself...

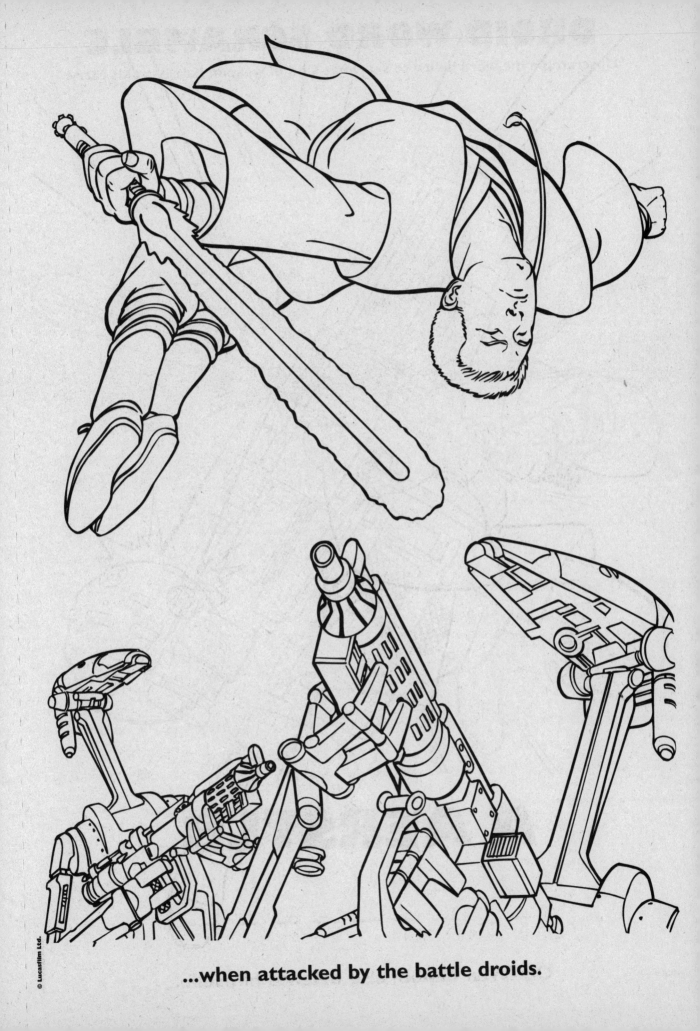

...when attacked by the battle droids.

DROID WORD SCRAMBLE

Unscramble the word below to see what kind of weapon battle droids carry.

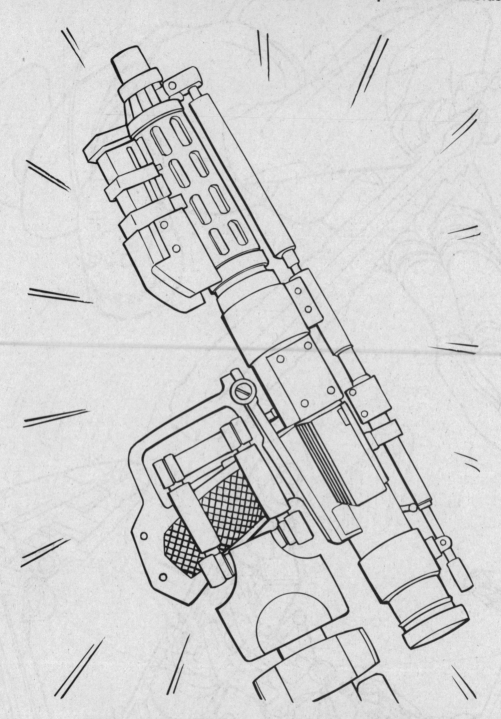

A AERSTLB

— — — — — — — —

Dalmatian Press

DROID WORD SCRAMBLE

Unscramble the word below to see what kind of droid is about to attack.

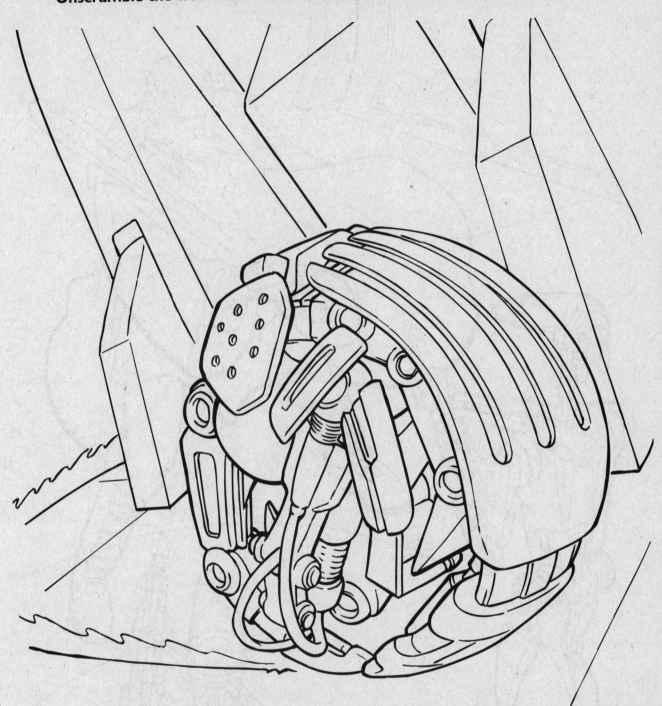

A ESTERDROY RODID

- -

Answer: A Destroyer Droid

Jedi never attack.

The Force flows through the Jedi.

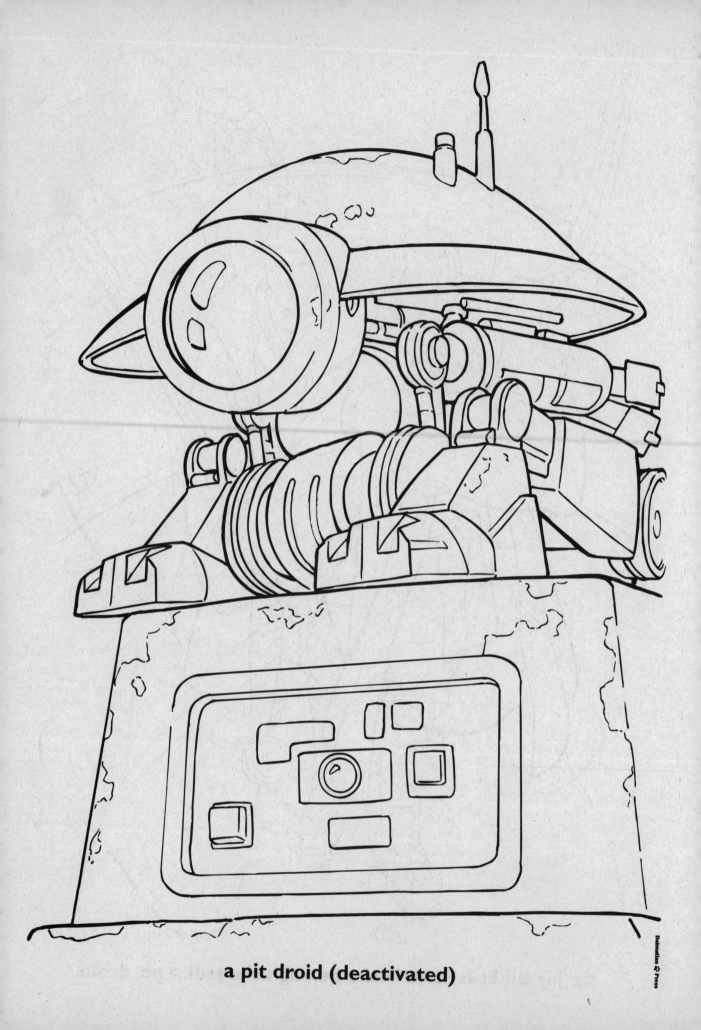

a pit droid (deactivated)

Dalmatian Press

Jar Jar is excited about making a new friend, the poweful Jedi Qui-Gon Jinn.

GUNGAN WORD SEARCH

How many times can you find the word "Jar Jar" in the grid below?

J	A	R	J	A	R
A	A	A	R	A	A
J	R	R	J	A	J
J	A	R	J	A	R
R	A	J	R	A	J
J	A	R	J	A	R

YOUR ANSWER: _____

Dalmatian Press

The Gungan warriors prepare for battle.

**Qui-Gon and Obi-Wan meet
Boss Nass, chief of the Gungans.**

He is called "Big Boss Nass" for a good reason.

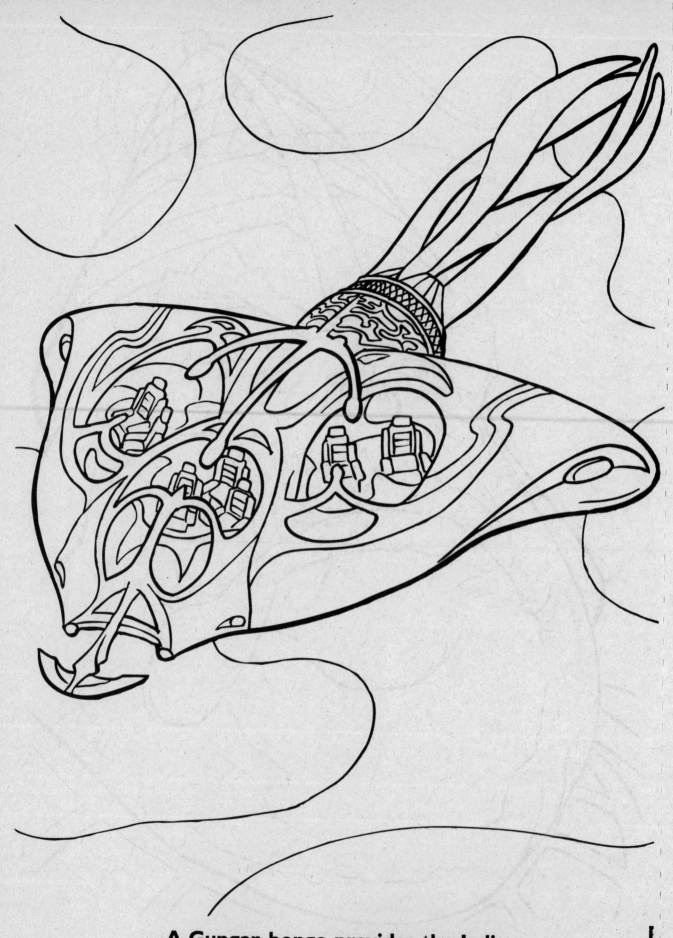

**A Gungan bongo provides the Jedi
with transport through the planet's core.**

There are many dangers going through the planet core, like this opee sea killer.

The opee sea killer attacks the Jedi in their bongo.

Watch out for the sando aqua monster.

THROUGH THE PLANET CORE

Help Qui-Gon, Obi-Wan and Jar Jar make
their way through the planet's core.

START

FINISH

Sea monsters are very dangerous!

A colo claw fish

MATCH EACH PICTURE TO THE CORRECT KIND OF SEA MONSTER.

1

2

3

A. COLO CLAW FISH

B. OPEE SEA KILLER

C. SANDO AQUA MONSTER

Answer: 1-B, 2-C, 3-A

"There's always a bigger fish...."

Jar Jar is frightened.

Anakin in the marketplace in Mos Espa.

Anakin leaves his mother.

Jar Jar is clumsy...

...and that annoys Sebulba.

Gungans prepare for battle.

"Meesa be tinkin weesa got a grand army..."

**Viceroy Nute Gunray communicates
with a hologram of Darth Sidious.**

**Darth Sidious commands his apprentice,
Darth Maul, to do his evil bidding.**

Qui-Gon Jinn ignites his lightsaber...

...in a spectacular duel with Darth Maul.

The battle rages on...

They cross lightsabers as they attack each other, trying to gain the upper hand.

FINISH DRAWING DARTH MAUL

Complete the rest of Darth Maul's face with your own drawing.

Darth Maul serves his master, Darth Sidious.

Obi-Wan joins the battle.

Darth Maul's lightsaber has two blades.

Darth Sidious uses the dark side of the Force.

**Qui-Gon, Obi-Wan and Anakin all use
the good side of the Force.**

© Lucasfilm Ltd.

**Obi-Wan Kenobi promises to train Anakin
in the ways of the Force.**

Yoda sits in his chair in the Jedi Council.

Mace Windu is a strong Jedi Master.

**The Jedi must deal with all sorts of characters
to keep peace in the galaxy.**

The Jedi Council members...

...are the strongest and wisest Jedi in the galaxy.

**Anakin Skywalker answers questions
from the Jedi Council.**

Mace Windu is a leader in the Jedi Council.

**The imposing Saesee Tiin and the beautiful
Depa Billaba are members of the Jedi Council.**

**Eeth Koth and Adi Gallia
are also members of the Jedi Council.**

Yarael Poof, Jedi Council member

Ki-Adi-Mundi, Jedi Council member

A lightsaber is the weapon of the Jedi.

A Jedi apprentice is called a Padawan learner.

Anakin Skywalker is a skilled pilot.

He is the only human who can control a Podracer.

"NOW, THIS IS PODRACING"

How many times can you find the word "POD" in the grid below?

P	O	D	D	O	P
D	O	P	P	O	D
P	O	D	D	O	P
D	D	P	D	P	D
P	O	D	D	O	P
D	P	P	O	D	P

YOUR ANSWER: _____

Dalmatian Press

START YOUR ENGINES

Help Ben Quadinaros get through the maze to his pod before the race starts!

START

FINISH

Pit droids help work on the Podracers.

**The pilots get excited before
the Boonta Eve Classic Podrace.**

Fode and Beed are the announcers at the Mos Espa Grand Arena.

Pit droids prepare for the big race.

MATCH EACH PICTURE TO THE CORRECT CHARACTER FROM THE PODRACE.

I

A. SEBULBA

2

B. FODE

3

C. BEED

Dalmatian Press

D. ANAKIN
SKYWALKER

E. PIT DROID

F. BEN
QUADINAROS

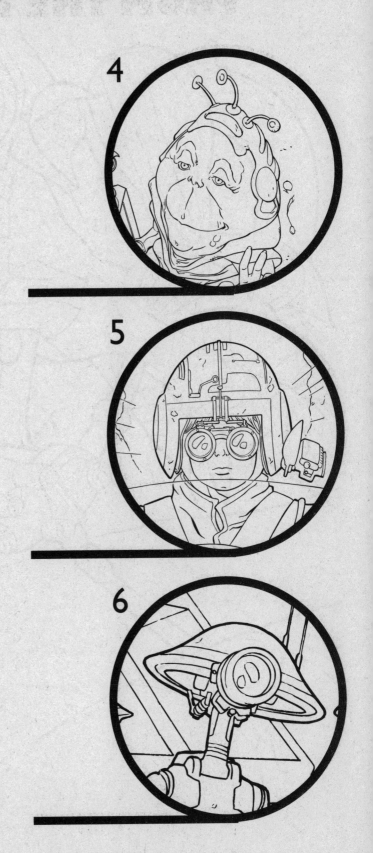

4

5

6

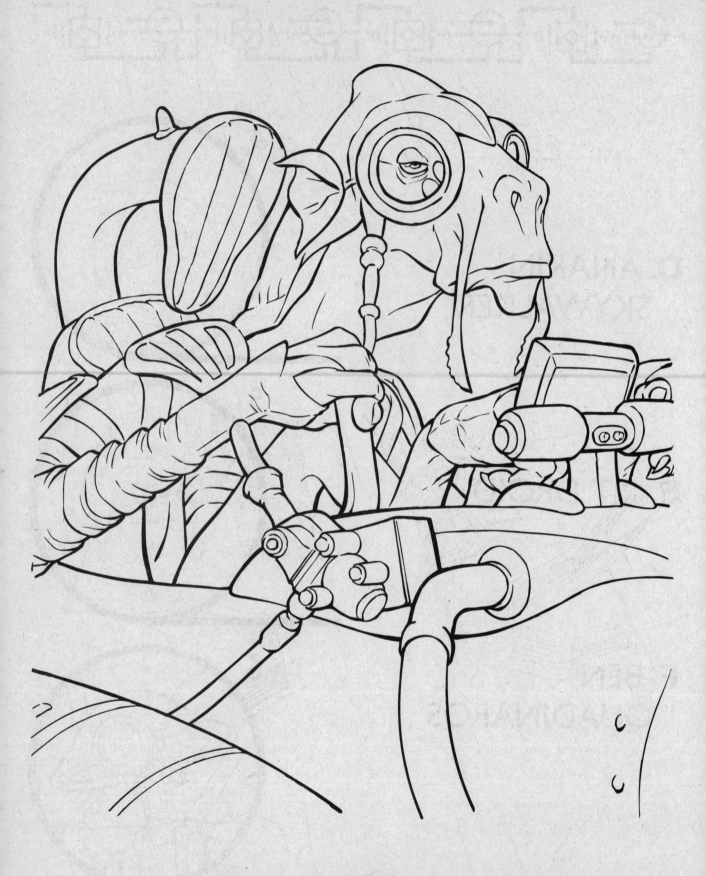

Sebulba will do anything to win the Podrace.

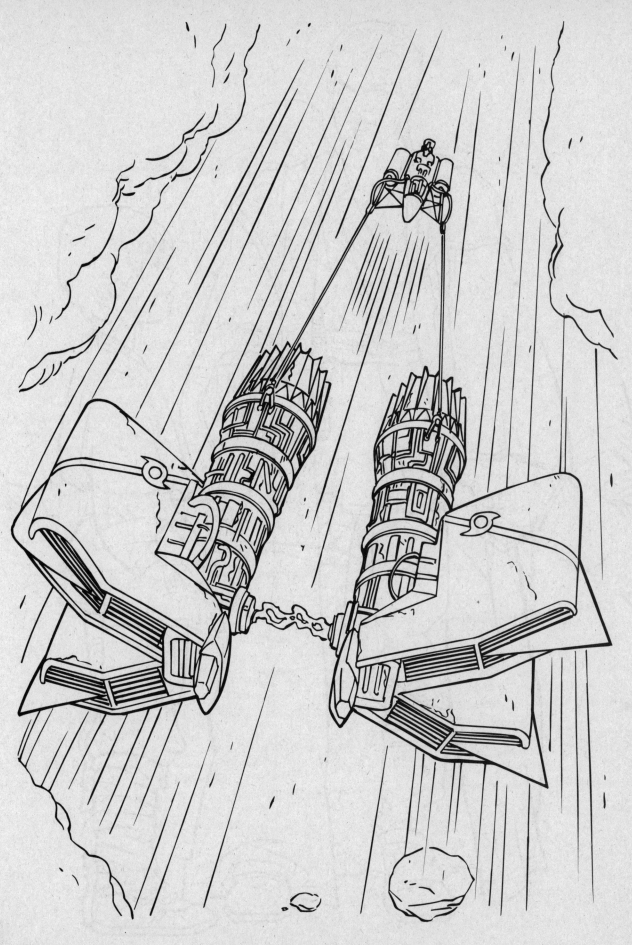

"He always wins...."

Obi-Wan Kenobi meets Anakin Skywalker.

THE BATTLE OF NABOO

How many Naboo starfighters do you count?

Your answer: _____

Answer: 24

This is Ben Quadinaros' first Podrace.

Hopefully his pod's energy coupling will hold together.

LOOKING AT ALL THE PODRACERS...

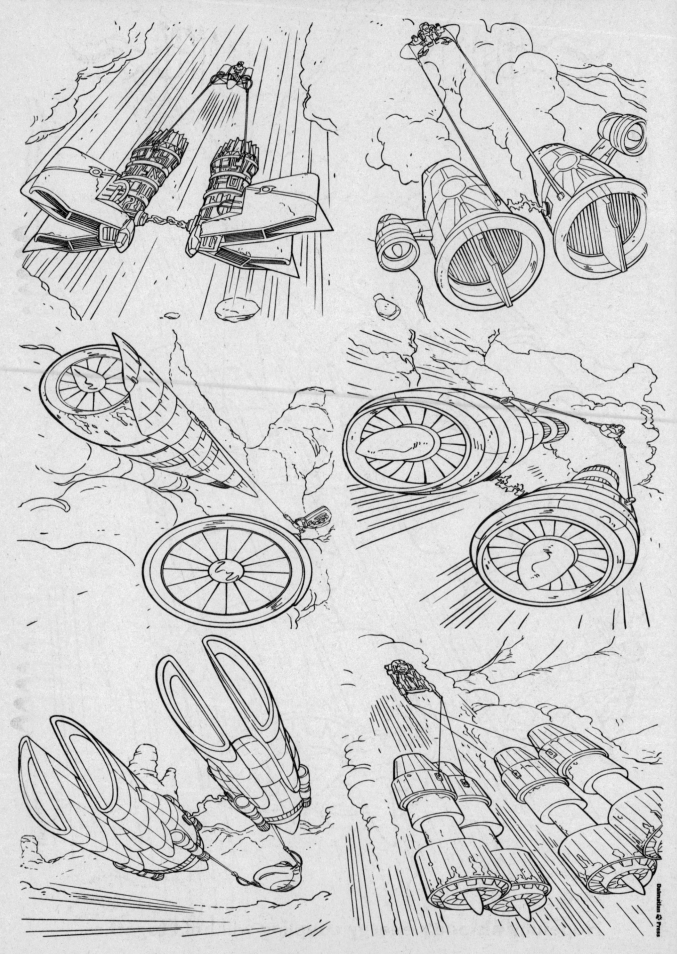

...DRAW YOUR OWN PODRACER BELOW.

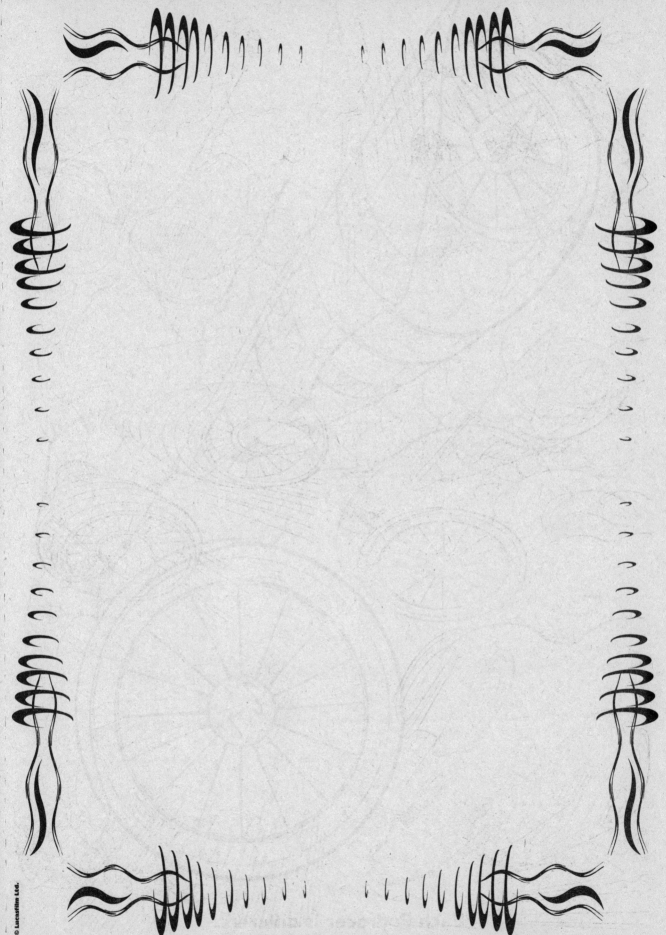

Each Podracer is different.

They are made to go very fast.

Big engines...

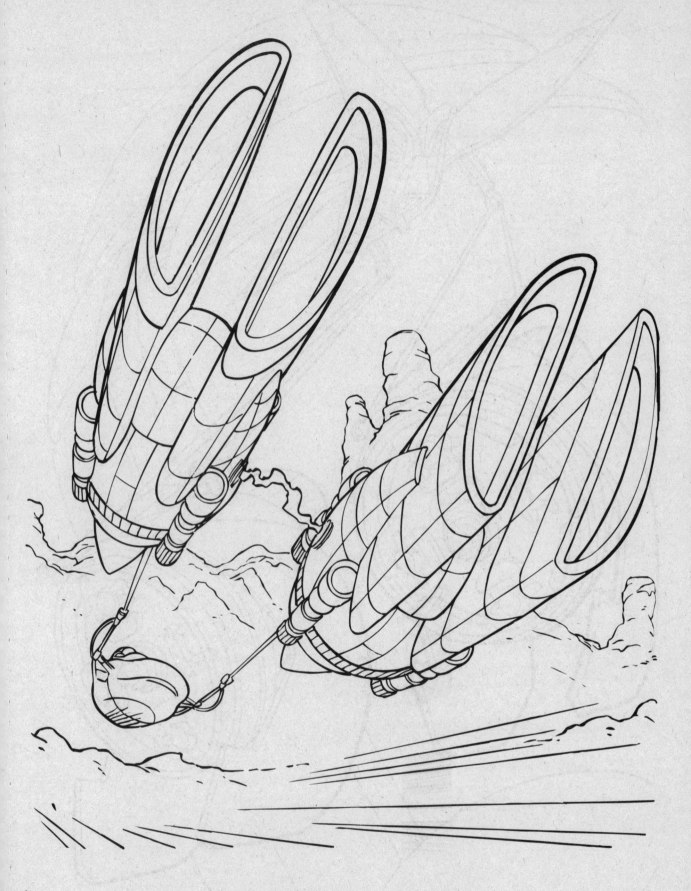

...pull the small pod along.

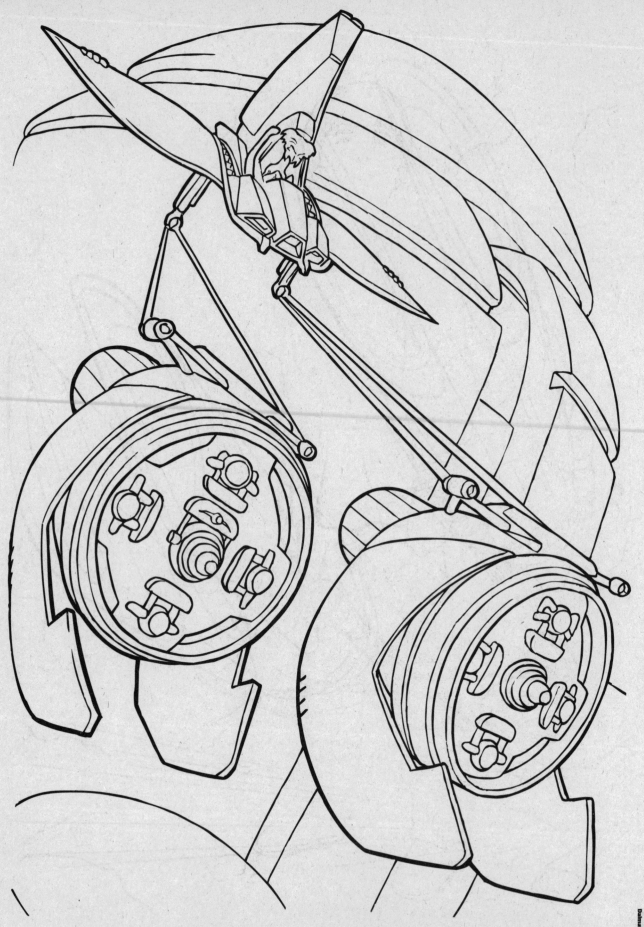

It is very dangerous to Podrace, illegal on most systems.

Anakin has special abilities; the Force is strong with him.

Anakin is a skilled pilot.

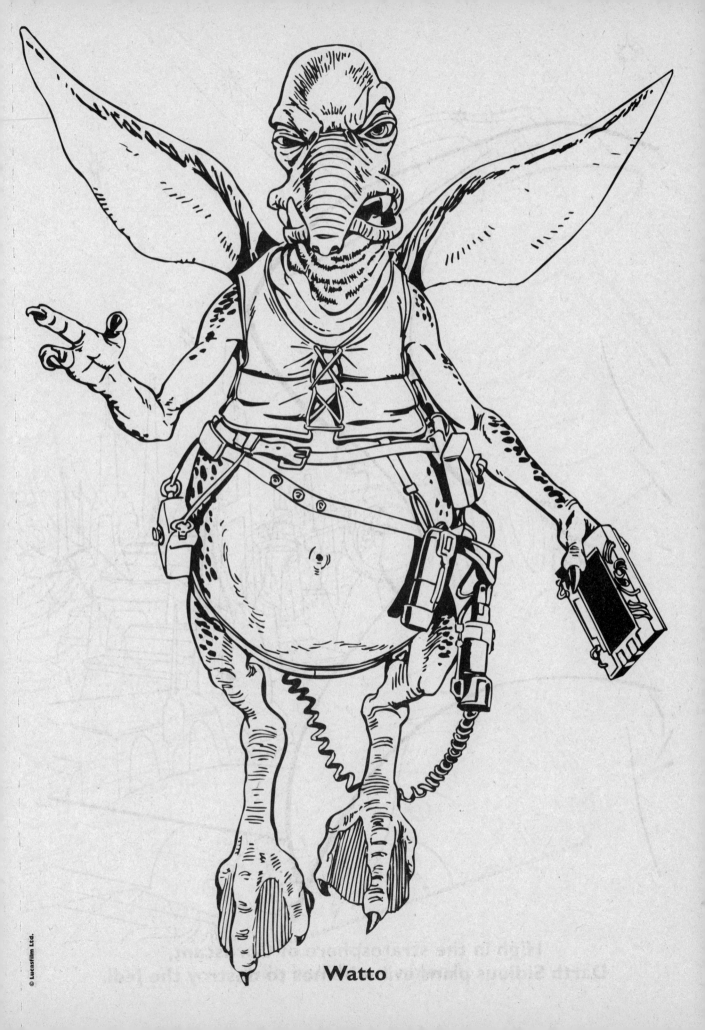

Watto

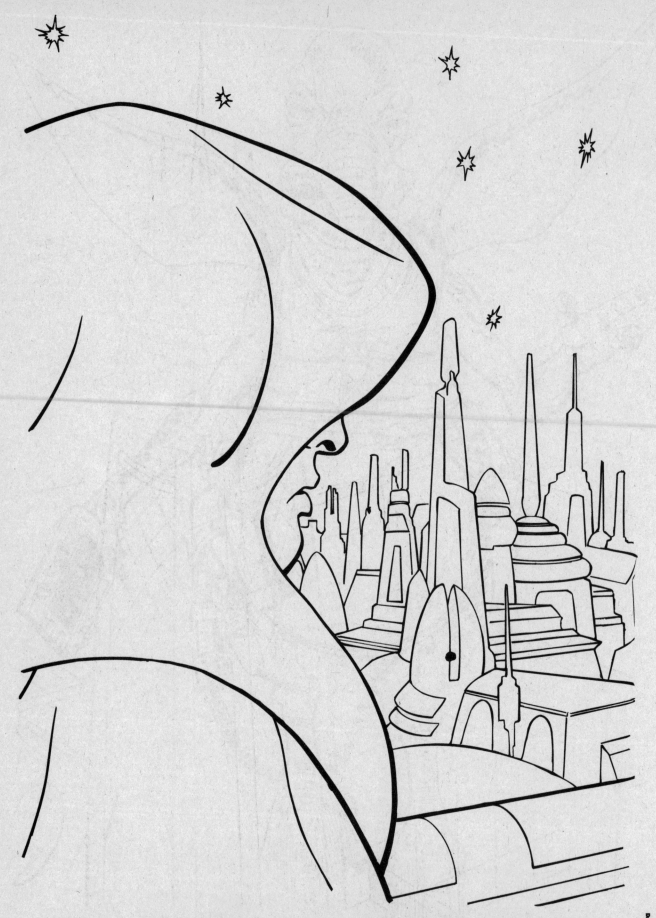

**High in the stratosphere of Coruscant,
Darth Sidious plans evil schemes to destroy the Jedi.**

The Jedi Temple is on Coruscant.

**Qui-Gon and Obi-Wan swim to where
the Gungans live under the water.**

Jar Jar leads them there.

"Wipe them out... all of them."

There can be only two Sith, a master and an apprentice.

Jedi have apprentices too.

Jedi are guardians of the peace in the galaxy.

Captain Tarpals will defend his home...

...against the invasion of the battle droids.

Anakin will race fairly... and win!

Sebulba will cheat... and lose.

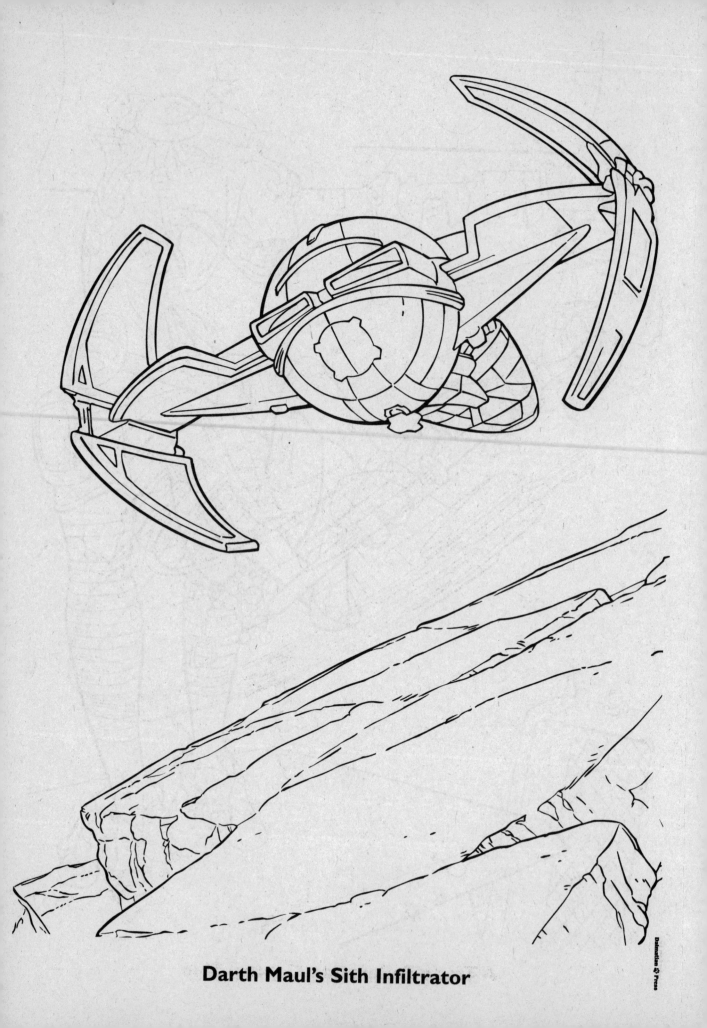

Darth Maul's Sith Infiltrator

A Trade Federation Control Ship

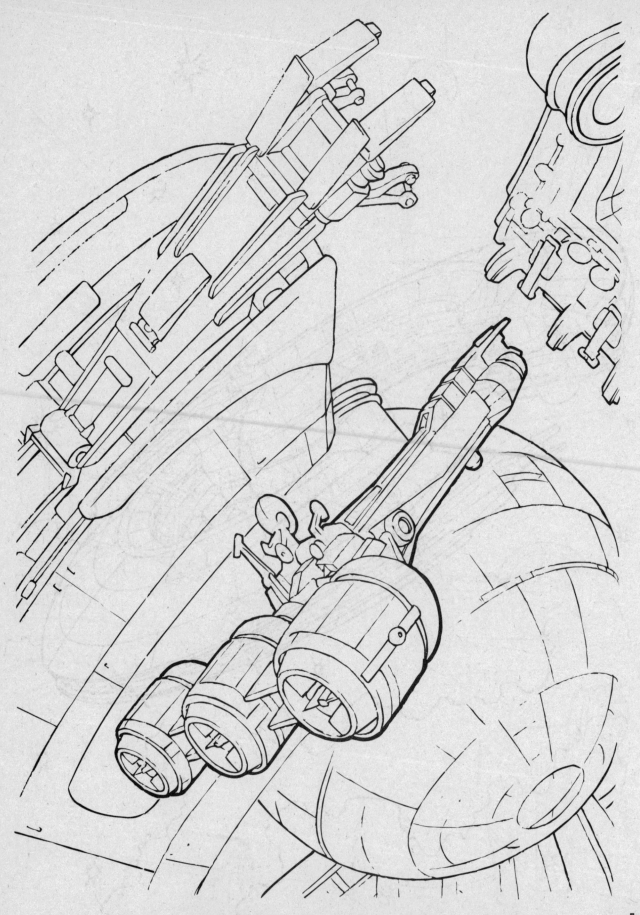

"Inform the Viceroy that the ambassadors wish to board immediately."

**The ambassadors' ship arrives in the hangar
of the Trade Federation Control Ship.**

**The Gungans use heavy weapons
to defend their home against the invasion.**

The battle droids have heavy weapons, too.

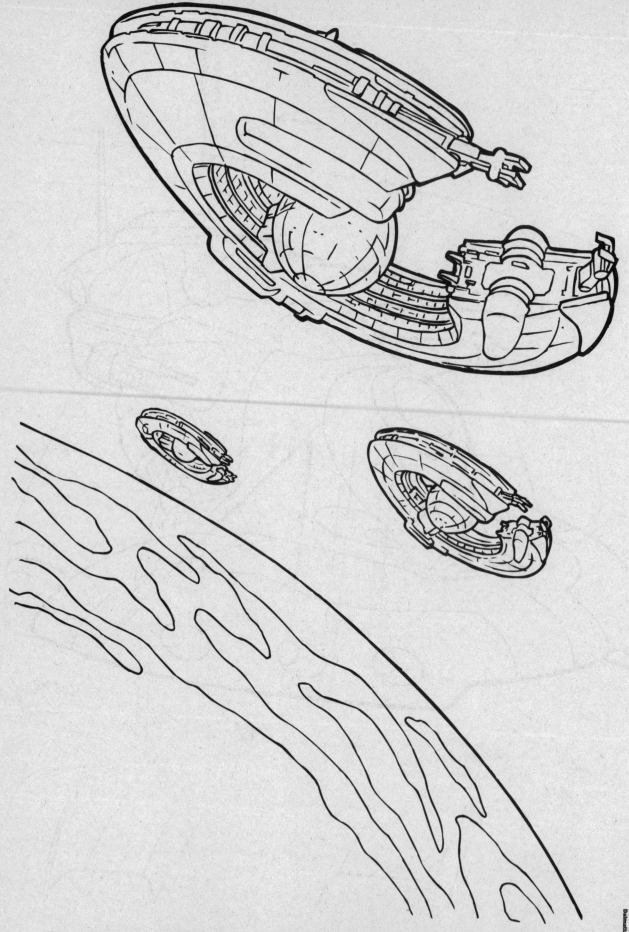

The Trade Federation controls the battle droid army.

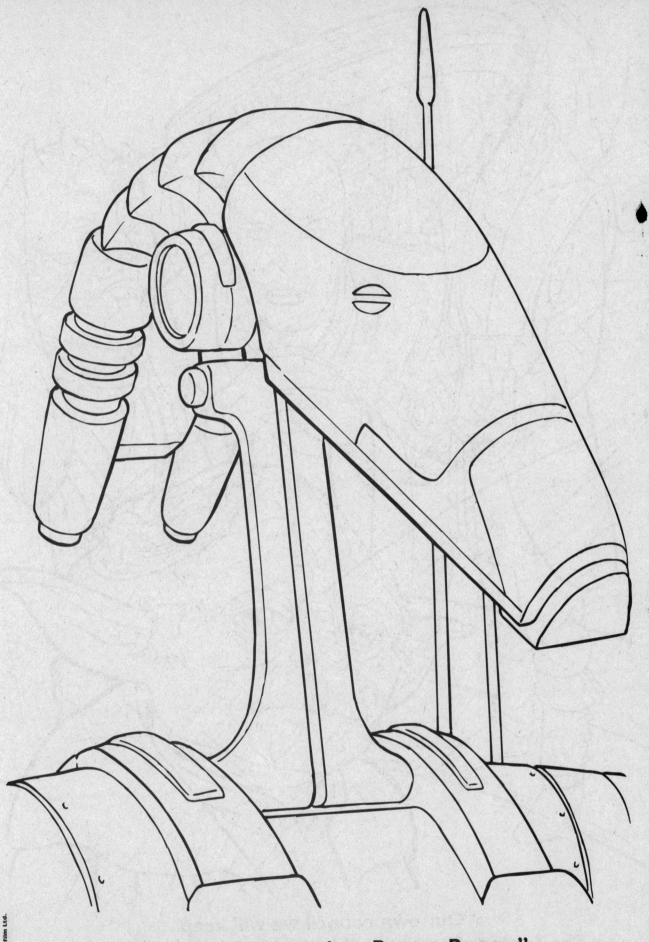

"Aye-Aye, Commander... Roger... Roger..."

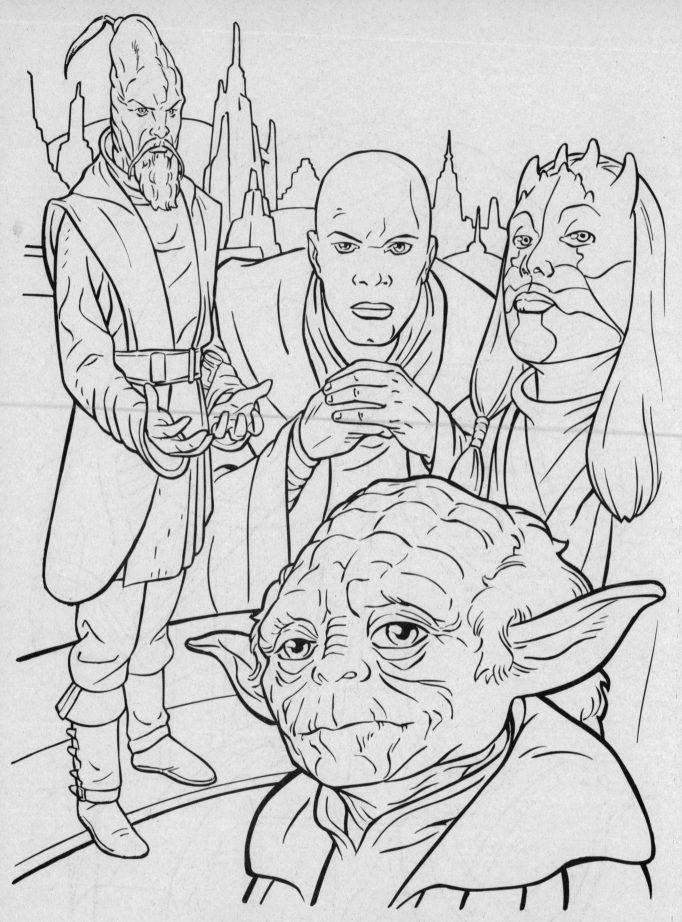

"Our own council we will keep
regarding who will be trained as a Jedi."

"Meesa thinks weesa being friends... Ha ha!"

The Queen makes a daring attempt to retake the palace.

Pilots run to their fighters to help in the battle.

USE THE GRID BELOW TO DRAW
R2-D2 & C-3PO
ON THE OPPOSITE PAGE.

WHO WAS THE LAST PERSON YODA TRAINED TO BE A JEDI?

A. OBI-WAN KENOBI

B. QUI-GON JINN

C. LUKE SKYWALKER

D. ANAKIN SKYWALKER

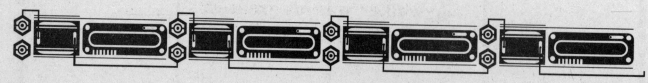

Answer: C.

IMPERIAL CROSSWORD PUZZLE

Down:

1. Senator from Naboo, later became Supreme Chancellor.
2. After becoming Supreme Chancellor, he declared himself _____.

Across:

3. Darth _____ helped him hunt down and destroy the Jedi.
4. As a young Padawan learner, Anakin Skywalker was his greatest _____.
5. He saw the Jedi as a _____ to his power.

Answers: 1. Palpatine, 2. Emperor, 3. Vader, 4. pupil, 5. threat

DRAW THE OTHER HALF OF ANAKIN IN HIS HELMET.

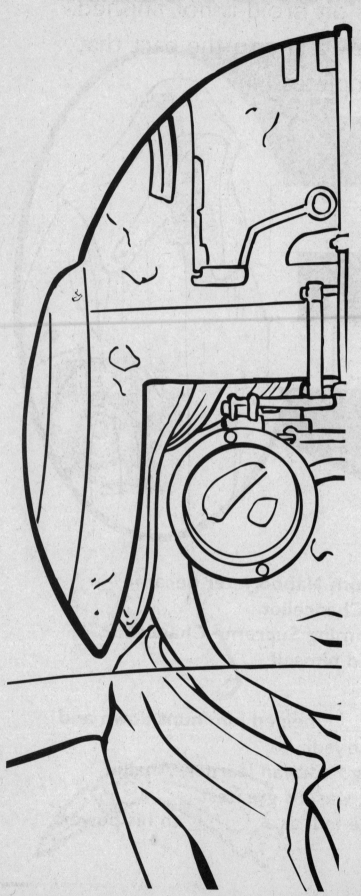

BUILD-A-BOT

This pit droid is not finished. Draw a line to the part that completes him.

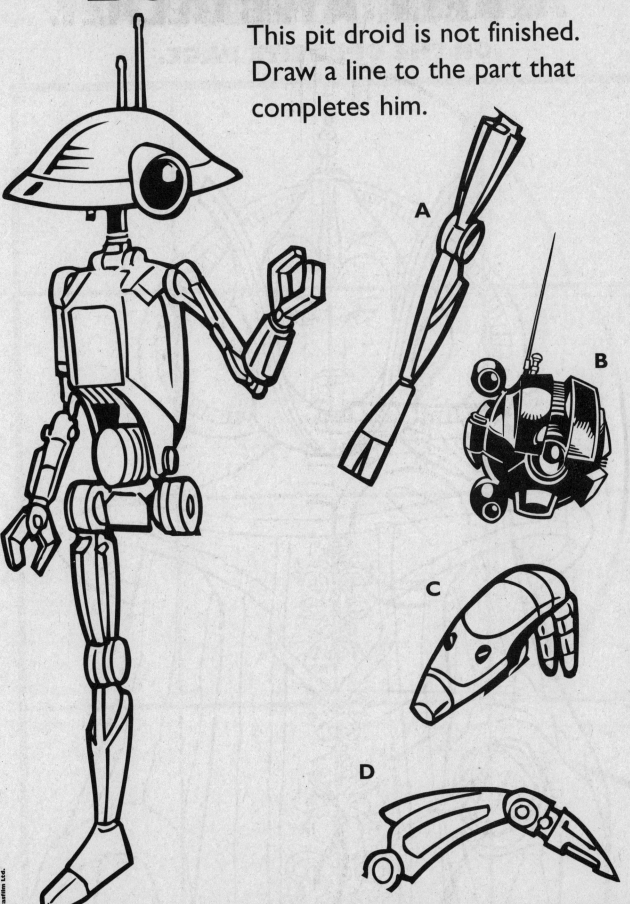

A

B

C

D

Answer: A

USE THE GRID BELOW TO DRAW
QUEEN AMIDALA
ON THE OPPOSITE PAGE.

ALDERAAN ESCAPE

**The Alderaan system has been hit by the Death Star laser.
Can you escape the maze before the planet is totaly destoyed?**

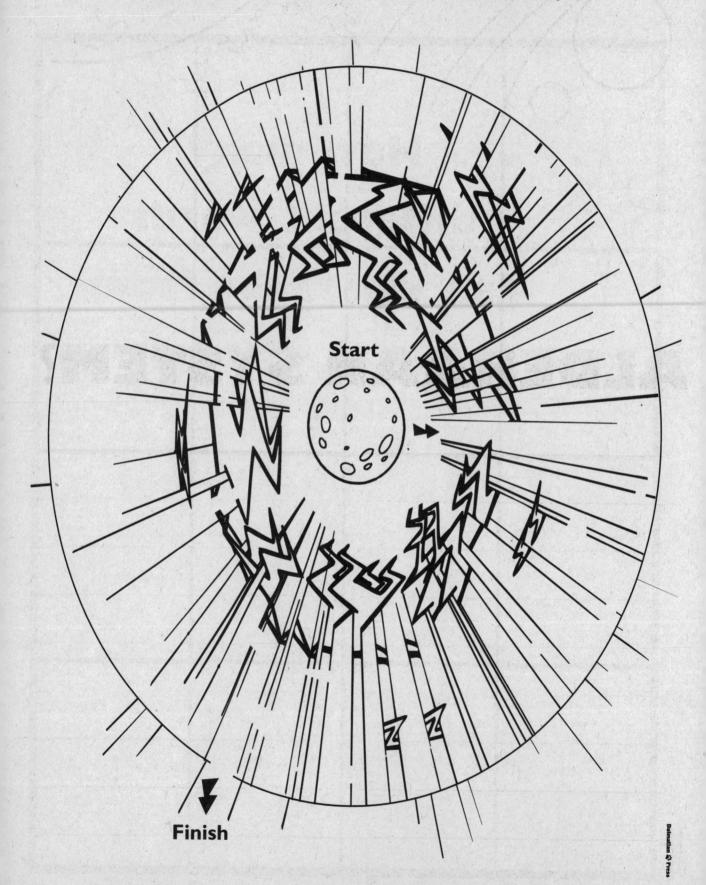

Start

Finish

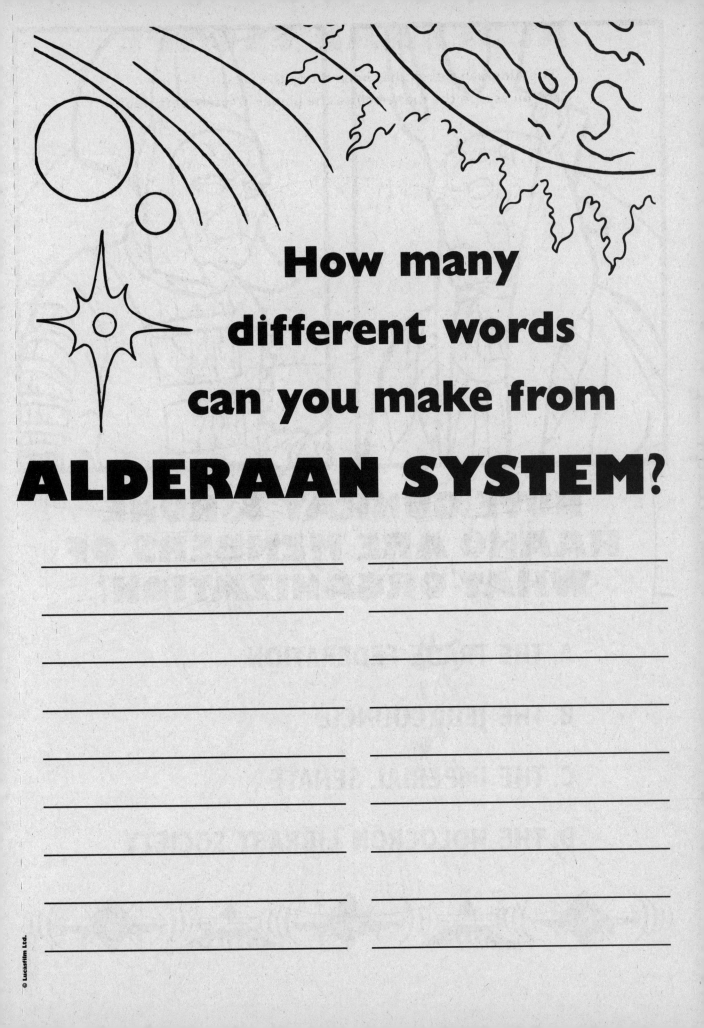

How many different words can you make from ALDERAAN SYSTEM?

NUTE GUNRAY & RUNE HAAKO ARE MEMBERS OF WHAT ORGANIZATION?

A. THE TRADE FEDERATION

B. THE JEDI COUNCIL

C. THE IMPERIAL SENATE

D. THE HOLOCRON LIBRARY SOCIETY

Dalmatian Press

BUILD-A-BOT

This battle droid is not finished. Draw a line to the part that completes him.

A

B

C

D

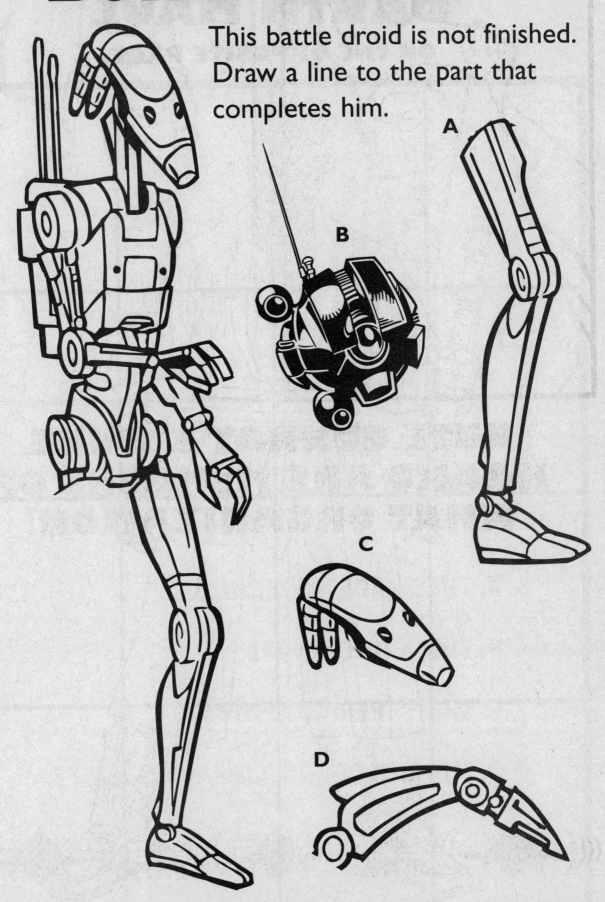

Answer: A

USE THE GRID BELOW TO DRAW
DARTH MAUL
ON THE OPPOSITE PAGE.

IMPERIAL WORD SEARCH

Look forwards, backwards, across, down and diagonally to find the words listed below:

The Force	dark side	TIE
Empire	Emperor	Vader
mask	evil	Senate
Death Star	X-wing	Ewok

V	B	D	F	E	W	O	K	R
S	A	H	J	M	A	S	K	A
E	L	D	L	P	N	P	T	T
N	I	V	E	E	R	I	T	S
A	V	O	S	R	E	Q	M	H
T	E	C	R	O	F	E	H	T
E	M	P	I	R	E	K	G	A
I	D	A	R	K	S	I	D	E
G	N	I	W	X	B	C	A	D

Dalmatian Press

TATOOINE SYSTEM CROSSWORD PUZZLE

Down:
1. Son of Darth Vader, raised on Tatooine by the Lars family.
2. Another name for Obi-Wan Kenobi.

Across:
1. The means of transport Luke uses to look for the droids.
3. Sand People _____ single file to hide their numbers.
4. Another name for Tusken Raiders.
5. Old wizard that lived as a hermit on Tatooine.
6. Obi-Wan has this color lightsaber.

Answers: 1. (down) Luke Skywalker; 2. Ben; 1. (across) landspeeder; 3. ride; 4. Sand People; 5. Obi-Wan Kenobi; 6. blue

JEDI WORD SCRAMBLE

Unscramble the words below and see Yoda's question to young Anakin.

WOH ELEF OUY?

_ _ _   _ _ _ _   _ _ _ ?

Dalmatian Press

REBEL ALLIANCE WORD SEARCH

Look forwards, backwards, across, down and diagonally to find the words listed below:

Lando	Luke	Skywalker
rebellion	Endor	fighter
Princess	Leia	Ackbar

N	H	X	I	O	E	J	F	S
P	O	F	K	D	Y	E	U	K
R	J	I	H	N	T	K	Z	Y
I	R	G	L	A	D	U	E	W
N	A	H	Q	L	R	L	V	A
C	B	T	L	P	E	W	E	L
E	K	E	O	I	A	B	M	K
S	C	R	A	C	N	I	E	E
S	A	B	H	E	N	D	O	R

TRADE FEDERATION
WORD SCRAMBLE

Unscramble the words below to see Darth Sidious' command to Nute Gunray.

PIWE MTEH TOU!

_ _ _ _ _ _ _ _ _ _ _ _

Dalmatian ✷ Press

DARTH MAUL'S WORD SCRAMBLE

Unscramble the words below to see what is special about Darth Maul's lightsaber.

OWT LABESD

_ _ _   _ _ _ _ _ _

Answer: Two blades

USE THE GRID BELOW TO DRAW
A DESTROYER DROID
ON THE OPPOSITE PAGE.

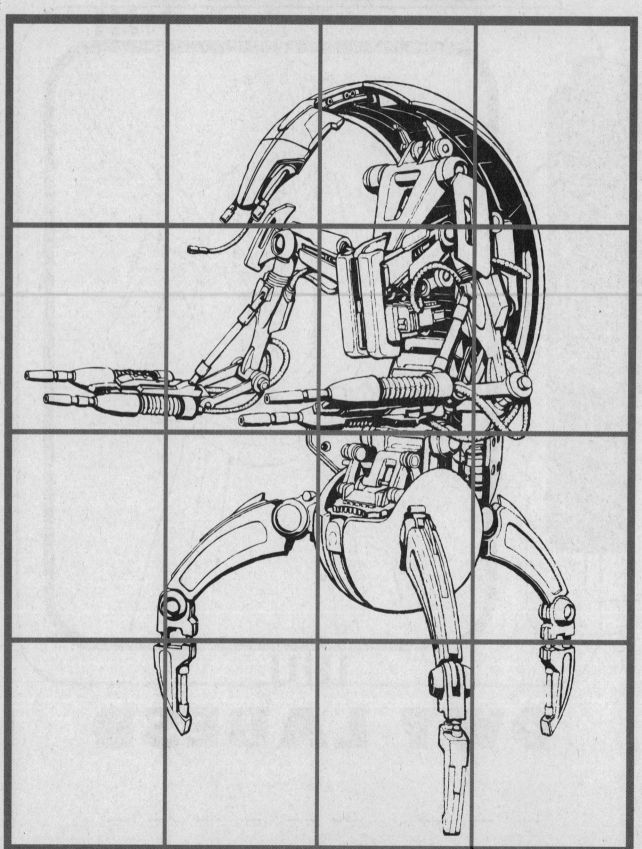

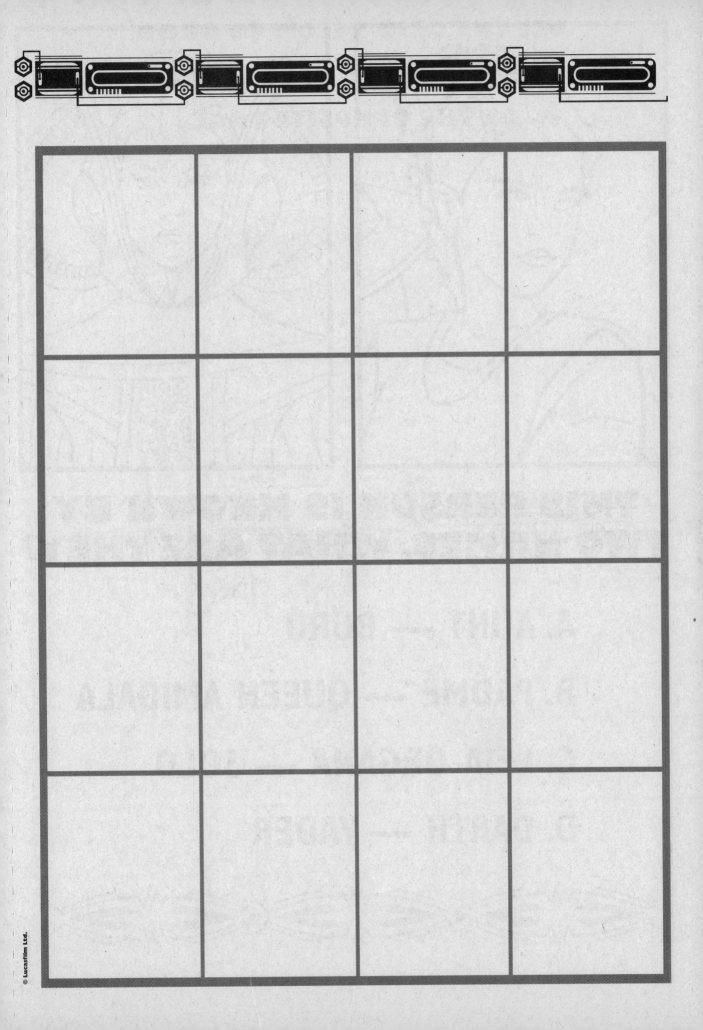

THIS PERSON IS KNOWN BY TWO NAMES. WHAT ARE THEY?

A. AUNT — BURU

B. PADMÉ — QUEEN AMIDALA

C. LEIA ORGANA — SOLO

D. DARTH — VADER

Dalmatian Press

QUEEN AMIDALA'S WORD SCRAMBLE

Unscramble the words below and see the Queen's first words to young Anakin.

RU'YOE A NUFYN

, _ _ _ _ _ _ _ _ _ _ _

TILTEL YOB.

_ _ _ _ _ _ _ _ _

Answer: You're a funny little boy.

JAWA'S WORD SEARCH

Look forwards, backwards, across, down and diagonally to find the words listed below:

Jawa   Tatooine   droid
Tusken   Raider   hooded
blaster   scavenger   short

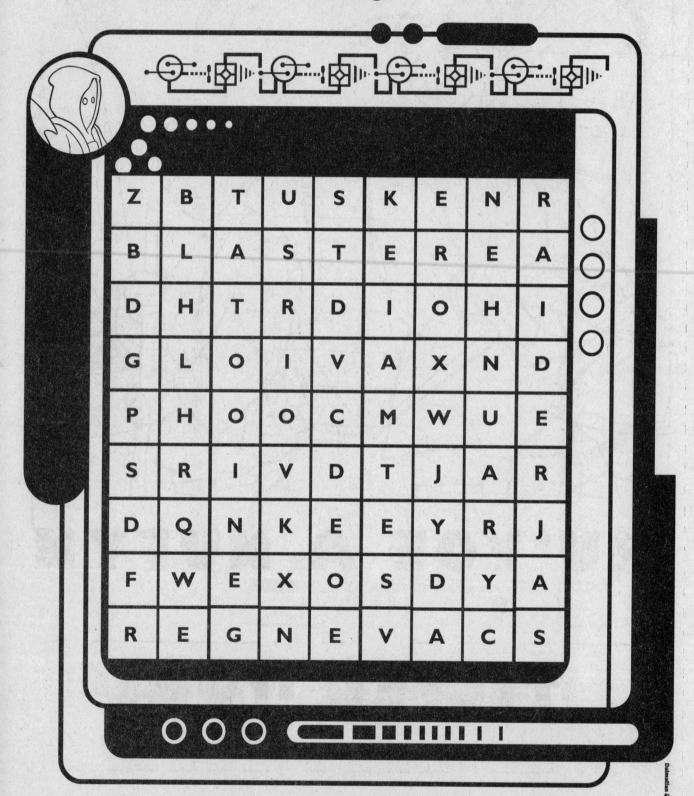

Z	B	T	U	S	K	E	N	R
B	L	A	S	T	E	R	E	A
D	H	T	R	D	I	O	H	I
G	L	O	I	V	A	X	N	D
P	H	O	O	C	M	W	U	E
S	R	I	V	D	T	J	A	R
D	Q	N	K	E	E	Y	R	J
F	W	E	X	O	S	D	Y	A
R	E	G	N	E	V	A	C	S

Dalmatian Press

DARTH VADER'S WORD SCRAMBLE

Unscramble the words below to read Vader's surprise for Luke during their duel.

I MA UORY THAFRE!

- - - - - - - - - - - - - - - - - -

THE JEDI ORDER

Which square completes the drawing?

A   B   C   D

Your answer: _____

Dalmatian Press

GUNGAN CROSSWORD PUZZLE

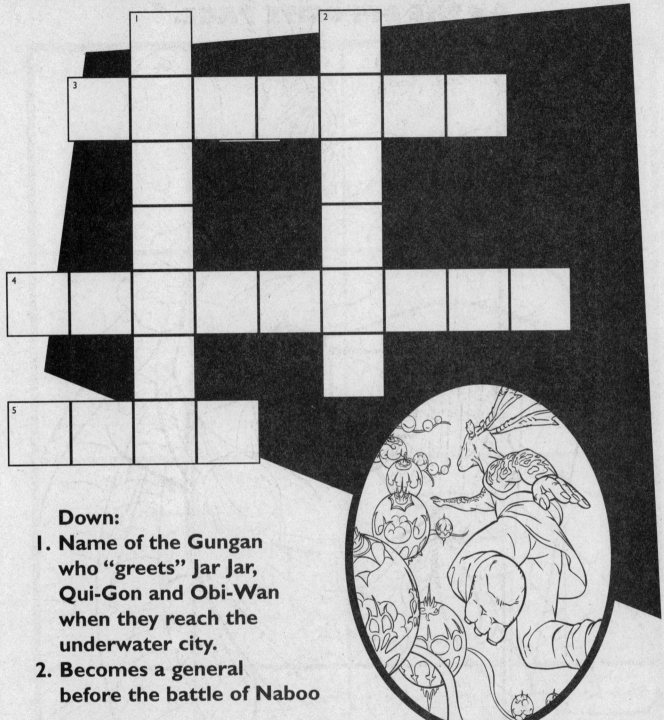

Down:
1. Name of the Gungan who "greets" Jar Jar, Qui-Gon and Obi-Wan when they reach the underwater city.
2. Becomes a general before the battle of Naboo

Across:
3. Tarpals rank in the military.
4. Another name for the Gungan military.
5. Leader of the Big Bosses.

Answers: 1. Tarpals, 2. Jar Jar, 3. Captain, 4. Grand Army, 5. Nass

USE THE GRID BELOW TO DRAW
JAR JAR BINKS
ON THE OPPOSITE PAGE.

WHO USES THESE KINDS OF FIGHTERS?

A. THE REBEL ALLIANCE - THE EMPIRE

B. TRADE FEDERATION - BANKING CLAN

C. JAWAS - SAND PEOPLE

D. BOUNTY HUNTERS - THE HUTTS

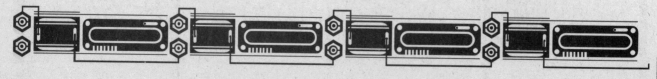

Answer: A

Dalmatian Press

ASTROMECH DROID REPAIRS

Which square completes the drawing?

A **B**  **C** **D**

Your answer: _____

WHO AM I?

CLUE: Padawan of Qui-Gon, promised to train young Anakin as a Jedi, hid the offspring of Skywalker, struck down in a lightsaber duel.

A. YODA

B. DARTH SIDIOUS

C. LUKE SKYWALKER

D. OBI-WAN KENOBI

Your answer:_____

Answer: D

Dalmatian Press

KAADU CORRAL

Which square completes the drawing?

A   B   C   D

Your answer: _____

Answer: B

CLONE TROOPER WORD SEARCH

Look forwards, backwards, across, down and diagonally to find the words listed below:

human
Kamino
Geonosis

clone
Jango
blaster

troops
Fett
rifle

358264983I

F	S	A	T	R	I	F	L	E
O	N	I	M	A	K	P	O	D
B	L	A	S	T	E	R	Y	A
J	A	N	G	O	F	E	T	T
Z	I	F	E	B	N	Q	R	J
H	U	M	A	N	U	O	A	T
L	O	N	E	E	O	S	E	N
H	Z	A	I	P	O	L	S	G
C	S	K	S	N	R	B	C	D

SWIMMING TO OTOH GUNGA

Which square completes the drawing?

A   B   C   D

Your answer: _____

WHO AM I?

CLUE: Senator representing Alderaan in the Imperial Senate, sister of Luke Skywalker, loves Han Solo, rescued from the Death Star.

A. QUEEN AMIDALA

B. JAR JAR BINKS

C. PRINCESS LEIA ORGANA

D. WATTO

Your answer: _____

Answer: C

Dalmatian Press

LUKE TO THE RESCUE

Which square completes the drawing?

A  B  C  D

Your answer: _____

Answer: B

USE THE GRID BELOW TO DRAW
R2-D2
ON THE OPPOSITE PAGE.

THESE DROIDS SHARE MANY ADVENTURES. WHO ARE THEY?

A. R5-D4 & TC-14

B. THX-1138 & A PIT DROID

C. A BATTLE & DESTROYER DROID

D. C-3PO & R2-D2

Dalmatian Press

DROID NAME SEARCH

Look forward, backward, across, down and diagonally to find the names listed below:

C-3PO   R2-D2   21-B
FX-7   R5-D4   R4-P17
IG-88   IT-O   K-3PO
ASN-121   4-LOM   CZ-3

D R O I D

n a m e s

4	3	Z	6	2	C	9	5	3
L	Q	R	2	D	2	8	2	2
O	I	Q	5	F	I	7	D	7
M	2	C	C	D	B	3	5	8
R	K	Z	O	3	4	4	O	8
4	3	C	O	7	P	C	5	G
P	P	O	X	6	2	O	T	I
I	O	F	3	Z	2	7	5	8
7	O	2	I	2	I	N	S	A

WHO AM I?

CLUE: Jedi Master and Council member, did not see Count Dooku as a threat, Jedi field commander in the first battle of the Clone Wars.

A. KI-ADI-MUNDI

B. EETH KOTH

C. ADI GALLIA

D. PLO KOON

Your answer: _____

Dalmatian Press

FASTEST SHIP IN THE GALAXY

Which square completes the drawing?

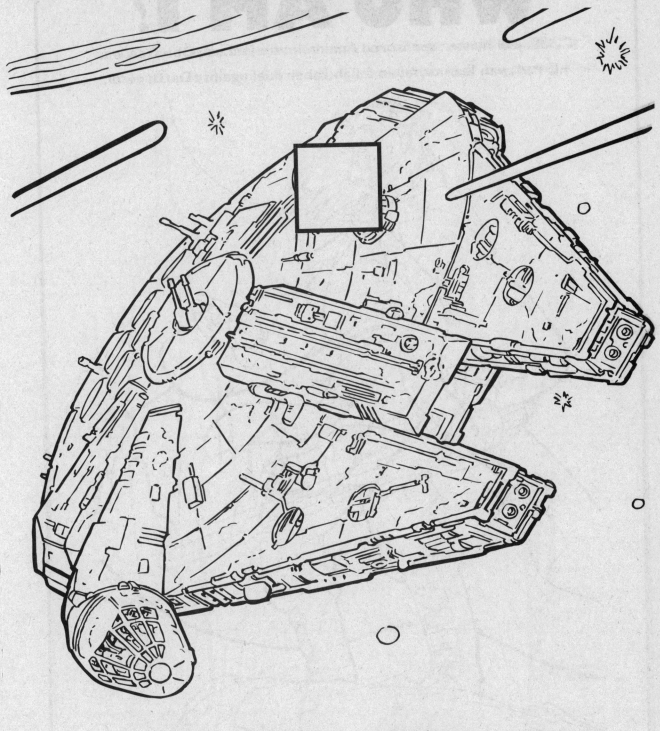

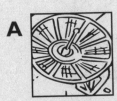 A  B  C   D

Your answer: _____

WHO AM I?

CLUE: Jedi Master, sponsored Anakin in the Podace, Obi-Wan was his Padawan learner, fell in a lightsaber duel against Darth Maul.

A. KI-ADI-MUNDI

B. QUI-GON JINN

C. SAESEE TIIN

D. PLO KOON

Your answer: _____

Dalmatian Press

WHO AM I?

CLUE: Dark and mysterious hooded warrior, skilled in the ways of the dark side of the Force, thought to be a Sith, apprentice to Darth Sidious.

A. DARTH SIDIOUS

B. DARTH VADER

C. DARTH TYRANUS

D. DARTH MAUL

Your answer: _____

DARK SIDE OF THE FORCE CROSSWORD PUZZLE

Down:

1. Last Sith apprentice to Emperor Palpatine.

Across:

2. _____ Skywalker, father of Luke.
3. The _____ are the sworn enemy of the Jedi.
4. Darth _____ is the Master of Darth Vader.
5. The color of Darth Vader's lightsaber.

Dalmatian Press

"THANK THE MAKER..."

Which square completes the drawing?

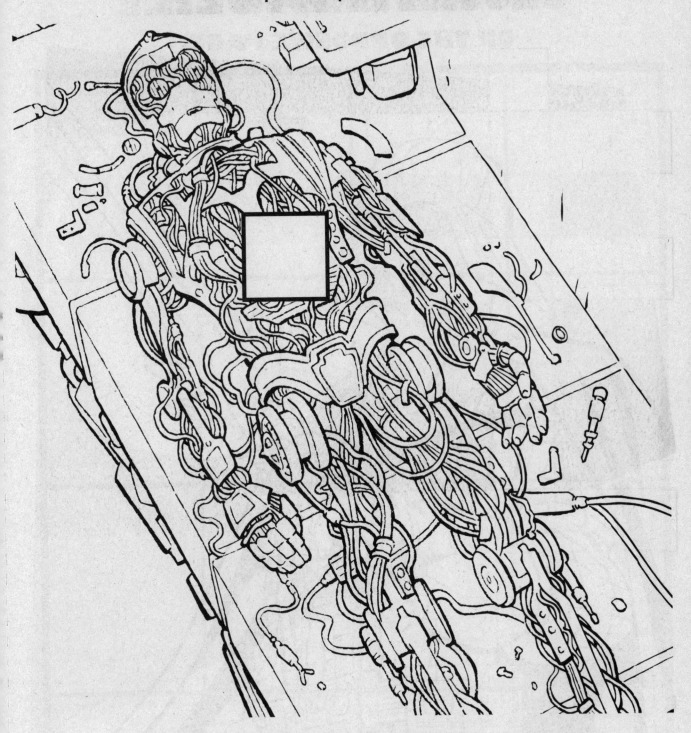

A 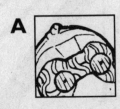 B  C  D

Your answer: _____

Answer: C

USE THE GRID BELOW TO DRAW
DARTH VADER
ON THE OPPOSITE PAGE.

Dalmatian Press

WHAT IS THE NAME OF THEIR PEOPLE?

A. THE JEDI OF CORUSCANT

B. THE KAMINOANS OF KAMINO

C. THE JAWAS OF TATOOINE

D. THE GUNGANS OF NABOO

Dalmatian Press

GENERAL JAR JAR
NEEDS A BOOMER

Which square completes the drawing?

A   B   C   D

Your answer: _____

Answer: D

ATTACK OF THE
CLONES

With a friend, take turns connecting the dots with a single straight line, up and down or left and right. When the connected lines complete a box, color that box with your color. When all the dots are connected and all the completed boxes colored, count the colored boxes. The trooper with the most colored boxes will advance in the Imperial Military to become a Republic Clone Trooper.

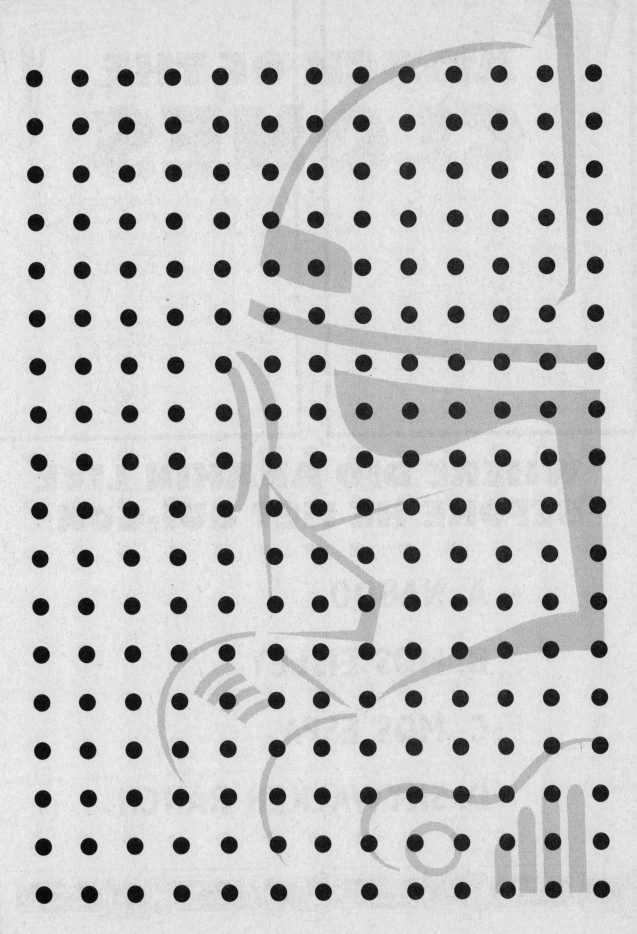

WHERE DID ANAKIN LIVE BEFORE HE MET QUI-GON?

A. NABOO

B. MOS EISLEY

C. MOS ESPA

D. SKYWALKER RANCH

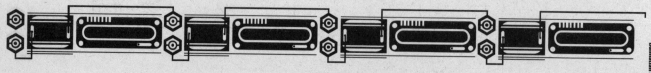

Dalmatian Press

THE FORCE FLOWS THROUGH A JEDI

Which square completes the drawing?

A   B   C   D

Your answer: _____

WHO AM I?

CLUE: Powerful Jedi Master, large hands, grim face, attended the funeral of Qui-Gon Jinn on Naboo, Council member.

A. SAESEE TIIN

B. YODA

C. MACE WINDU

D. JOCASTA NU

Your answer: _____

Dalmatian Press

WHAT FLOWS THROUGH A JEDI AND GIVES HIM STRENGTH?

A. LIFE BLOOD

B. ANCIENT WISDOM

C. BLUE LIGHTNING

D. THE FORCE

USE THE GRID BELOW TO DRAW
THE DEATH STAR
ON THE OPPOSITE PAGE.

WHY DOESN'T SEBULBA LIKE JAR JAR?

A. JAR JAR IS CLUMSY.

B. JAR JAR SPILLED SEBULBA'S LUNCH.

C. SEBULBA IS MEAN AND NASTY.

D. ALL OF THE ABOVE.

SQUASH YOU LIKE A DUG

Which square completes the drawing?

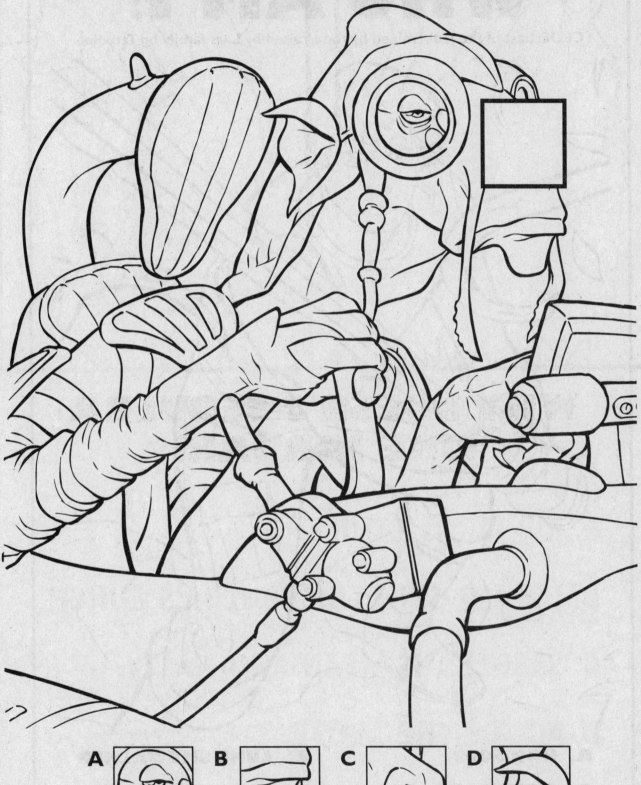

A B C D

Your answer: _____

Answer: C

WHO AM I?

CLUE: Last of the Jedi, trained by Yoda, raised by Lars family on Tatooine.

A. HAN SOLO

B. LUKE SKYWALKER

C. OWEN LARS

D. BEN KENOBI

Your answer: _____

Dalmatian Press

WHO AM I?

CLUE: Wookiee from Kashyyyk, friend and co-pilot of Han Solo.

A. JABBA THE HUTT

B. WATTO

C. CHEWBACCA

D. BOBA FETT

Your answer: _____

WHO AM I?

CLUE: Dark Lord of the Sith, hunted down and destoyed the Jedi.

A. DARTH SIDIOUS   **B. DARTH MAUL**

C. DARTH VADER   **D. DARTH TYRANUS**

Your answer: _____

Dalmatian Press

WHO AM I?

**CLUE: Killed by Anakin Skywalker on board
the second Death Star during the Battle of Endor.**

A. EMPEROR PALPATINE   **B. DARTH MAUL**

C. DARTH VADER   **D. DARTH TYRANUS**

Your answer: _____

Answer: A

USE THE GRID BELOW TO DRAW
THE MILLENNIUM FALCON
ON THE OPPOSITE PAGE.

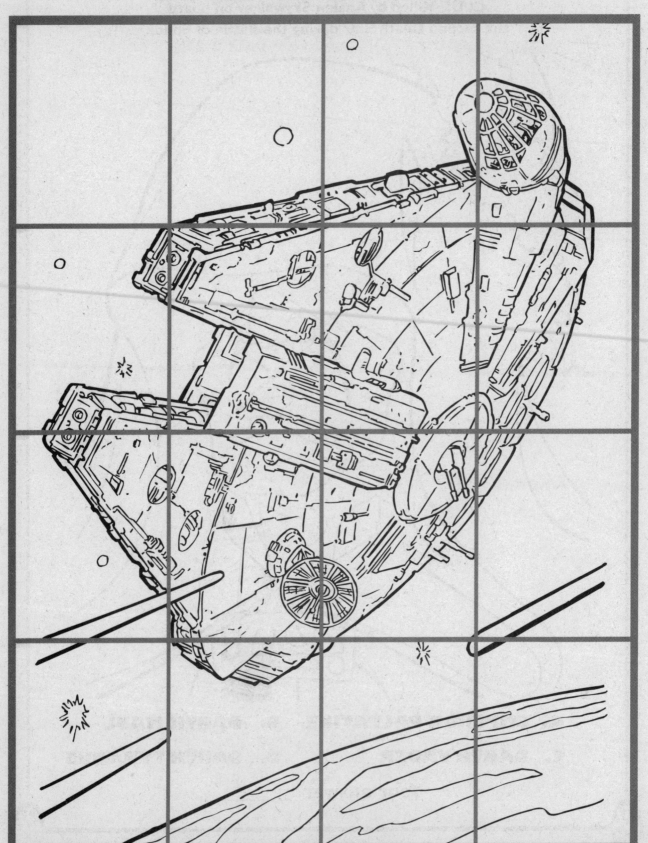

WHO AM I?

CLUE: The *Millennium Falcon* belongs to him, Chewbacca is his first mate.

A. HAN SOLO

B. LUKE SKYWALKER

C. OWEN LARS

D. BEN KENOBI

Your answer: _____

Dalmatian Press

WHO AM I?

CLUE: Very old, small but powerful Jedi Master, has a green lightsaber and pointy ears.

A. YODA

B. YADDLE

C. WATTO

D. JANGO FETT

Your answer: _____

Answer: A

SPELL-A-DROID MAZE

Follow the path through the maze that spells "C-3PO."

START

FINISH

DETENTION BLOCK 1138

Lead our heroes through the maze to rescue the princess.
Be sure to pick up each character along the way.

START

FINISH

WHO AM I?

CLUE: Served as Queen and Senator from the Naboo system.

A. YADDLE

B. BERU LARS

C. AMIDALA

D. PRINCESS LEIA

Your answer: _____

Dalmatian Press

WHO AM I?

CLUE: Faithful protocol droid of the Trade Federation Viceroy.

A. TC-14

B. R2-D2

C. C-3PO

D. R5-D4

Your answer: _____

Answer: A

WHERE IS
GUNGAN CITY LOCATED?

A. IN THE CLOUDS ON BESPIN

B. UNDER WATER ON NABOO

C. IN THE DESERT ON TATOOINE

D. THE FOREST MOON ENDOR

Dalmatian Press

THERE'S ALWAYS A BIGGER FISH

Which square completes the drawing?

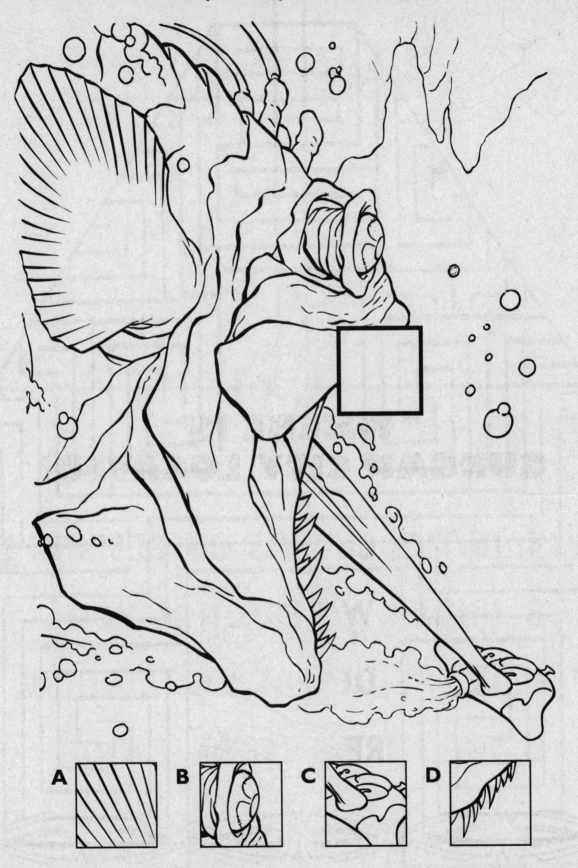

Your answer: _____

JABBA'S PALACE MAZE

Help Watto find his way through the maze to place his bet with Jabba the Hutt.

START

FINISH

Dalmatian Press

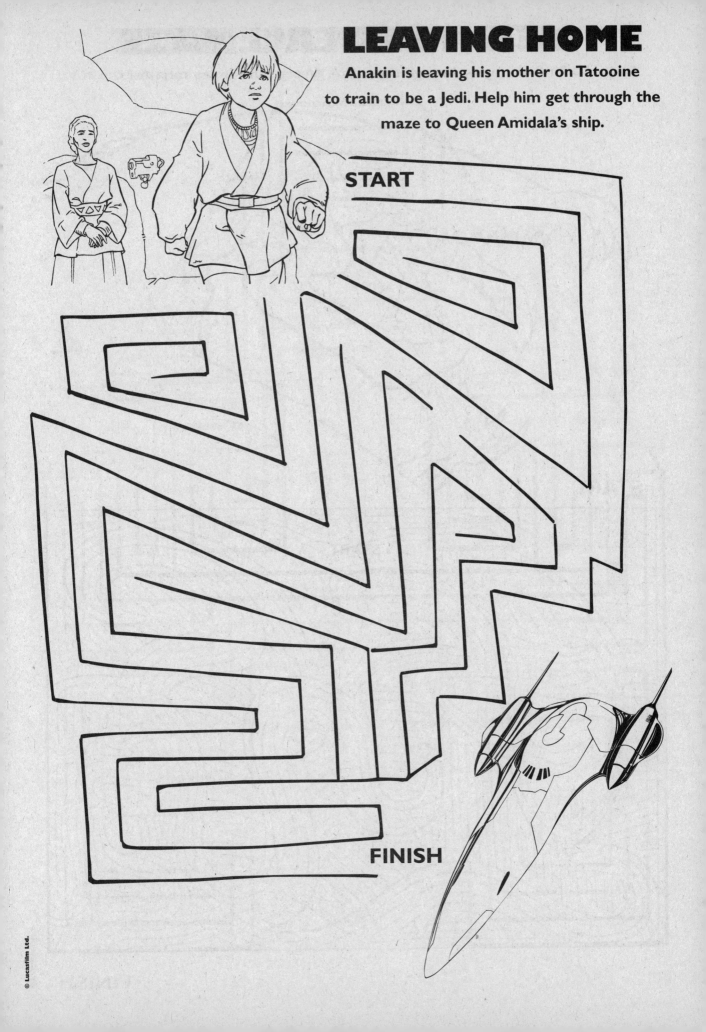

LEAVING HOME

Anakin is leaving his mother on Tatooine to train to be a Jedi. Help him get through the maze to Queen Amidala's ship.

START

FINISH

SEA MONSTER'S MAZE

Find your way through the maze. Watch out for sea monsters.

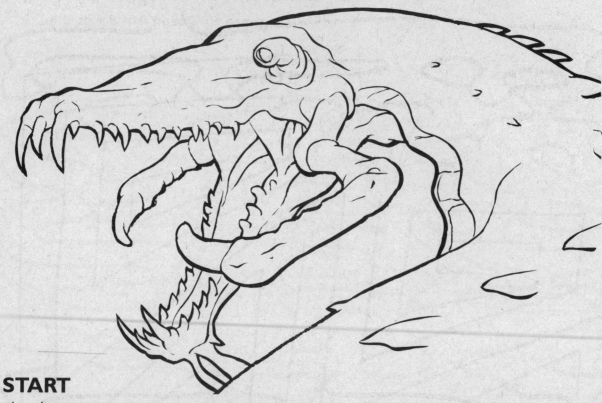

START

FINISH

"BIG GUBBA FISH..."

Swim through the undersea maze to see what Jar Jar is so afraid of.

START

FINISH

VADER'S MAZE

Activate Darth Vader's life support by making your way through the maze on his chest plate.

START

FINISH

ACTIVATE!

Dalmatian Press

LOST PIT DROID

The Podrace is about to start.
Help the pit droid get through the maze and back to his crew.

START

FINISH

WHEN THESE TWO DUEL, WHO WINS?

A. OBI-WAN KENOBI

B. QUI-GON JINN

C. DARTH MAUL

D. BAIL ORGANA

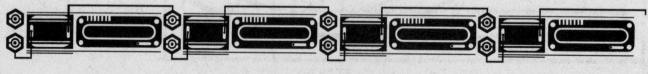

Answer: A

REBEL ALLIANCE MAZE

Lead your squadron of X-wing fighters back to their secret Rebel base.

FINISH

START

EMERGENCY COUNCIL

Help Jedi Master Yarael Poof through the maze and back to the Jedi temple for an emergency meeting of the Jedi Council.

FINISH

START

WHAT PLANET ARE THESE ANIMALS FROM?

A. CORUSCANT

B. NABOO

C. DAGOBAH

D. TATOOINE

EVERYONE ABOVE IS A MEMBER OF WHAT ORGANIZATION?

A. THE SITH

B. THE JEDI COUNCIL

C. THE BANKING CLAN

D. THE SENATE

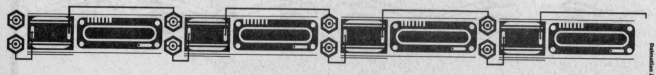

Dalmatian Press

DARK SIDE OF THE FORCE MAZE

Use the good side of the Force to navigate your way through the depths of the dark maze.

START

FINISH

© Lucasfilm Ltd.

THE DEATH STAR PLANS

Help the Rebellion against the Empire by making your way
through the Death Star schematic and finding a flaw in the defense mechanisms.

START

FINISH

WHO TAKES TIME DURING THEIR DUEL TO MEDITATE?

A. OBI-WAN KENOBI

B. QUI-GON JINN

C. DARTH MAUL

D. KI-ADI-MUNDI

Answer: A

OBI-WAN IS QUI-GON'S _____.

A. FRIEND AND PUPIL

B. PADAWAN LEARNER

C. LAST HOPE TO TRAIN ANAKIN

D. ALL OF THE ABOVE

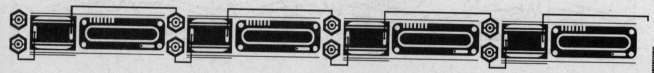

Dalmatian Press

THE WEAPON OF A JEDI

Which square completes the drawing?

A   B   C   D

Your answer: _____

Answer: D

USE THE GRID BELOW TO DRAW
AN X-WING FIGHTER
ON THE OPPOSITE PAGE.

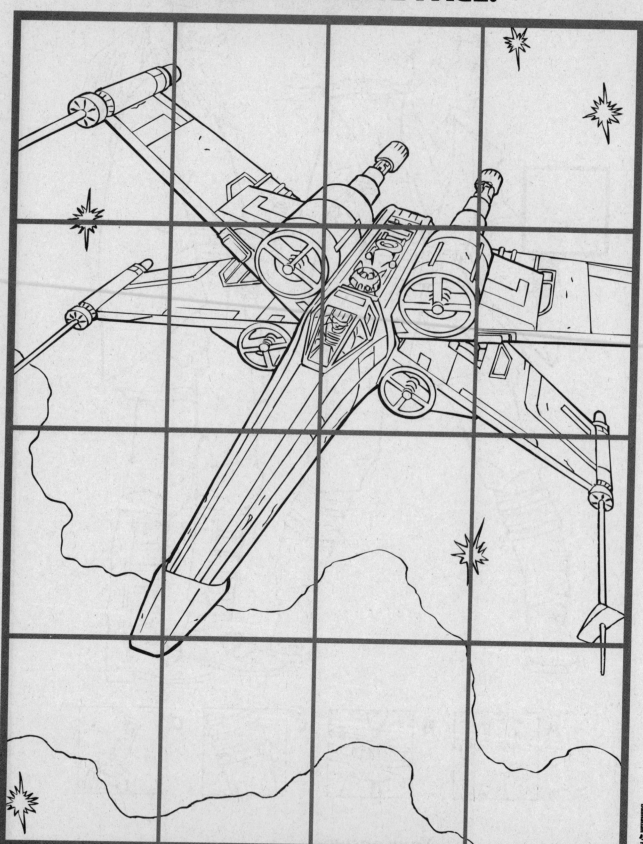

Dalmatian Press

SPILLED SOUP

Sebulba is frustrated with Jar Jar for spilling his soup.

Help Sebulba find Jar Jar before he gets away.

STAR WARS MAZE

Find your way through the maze to a "galaxy far, far away...."

START

FINISH

ASTROMECH DROID MAZE

It's good to have a few astromech droids on board your ship if you get lost.

With the droids' help, navigate your way through the complex maze.

START

FINISH

DARTH MAUL'S MAZE

Defeat Darth Maul by solving his complex Sith maze.

START

FINISH

DARTH SIDIOUS' EVIL MAZE

Use the Force to navigate your way through Darth Sidious' evil maze.

Only a Jedi, with the Force as his ally, will succeed.

START

FINISH

SPELL-A-DROID MAZE

Go through the maze along the path that spells "battle" droid.

START

FINISH

SPELL-A-GUNGAN MAZE

Go through the maze along the path that spells Captain "Tarpals."

START

FINISH

TIE FIGHTER VS. X-WING MAZE

FINISH

START

DARTH MAUL'S SITH INFILTRATOR

Only a Sith could navigate through this maze.

START

FINISH

SPELL-A-JEDI MAZE

Go through the maze along the path that spells "Yoda."

START

FINISH

SPELL-A-DUG MAZE

Go through the maze along the path that spells "Sebulba."

START

FINISH

DARTH VADER'S MAZE

Use the Force to navigate your way through Darth Vader's maze.
Only a Jedi, with the Force as his ally, will succeed.

START

FINISH

USE THE GRID BELOW TO DRAW
A SQUADRON OF TIE FIGHTERS
ON THE OPPOSITE PAGE.

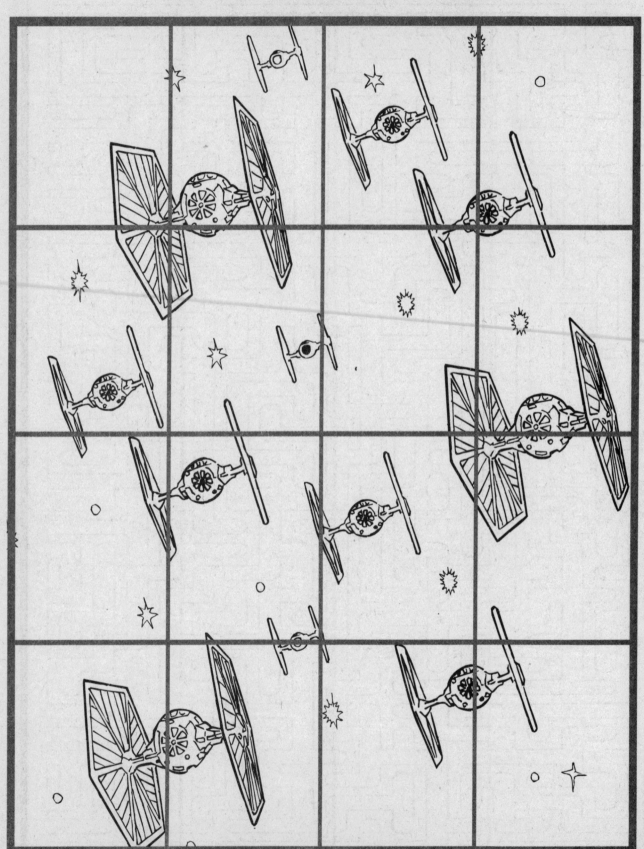

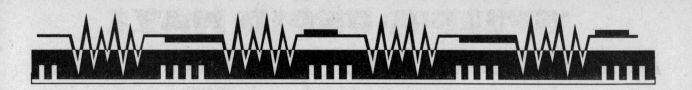

SPELL-A-DROID MAZE

Go through the maze along the path that spells "R2-D2."

START

FINISH

DROID CROSSWORD PUZZLE

Down:

1. R2-D2 is an _____ droid.

Across:

2. Droid that can generate its own deflector shield.
3. Astromech droid that helps the Queen's ship slip past the Trade Federation blockade.
4. An _____ probe droid was destroyed by Han Solo on Hoth.
5. A protocol droid built by Anakin Skywalker.

Answers: 1. astromech, 2. destroyer, 3. R2-D2, 4. Imperial, 5. C-3PO

WHO DO THE BATTLE DROIDS AND DESTROYER DROIDS FIGHT FOR?

A. THE REPUBLIC

B. THE TRADE FEDERATION

C. THE JEDI

D. THE CLONE ARMY

Dalmatian Press

SPELL-A-DROID MAZE

Go through the maze along the path that spells "pit" droid.

START

FINISH

SPELL-A-QUEEN MAZE

Go through the maze along the path that spells Queen "Amidala."

START

FINISH

BLAST 'EM

Which square completes the drawing?

A **B** **C** **D**

Your answer: _____

Answer: C

THE SMUGGLER'S CROSSWORD PUZZLE

Down:

1. Mighty Wookiee, co-pilot of the *Millennium Falcon*.
2. _____ hunters are after Han for the price on his head.

Across:

3. Princess Leia once described him as a "scruffy-looking nerf herder."
4. The ship that made the Kessel Run in less time than any other, the *Millennium* _____.
5. Vile gangster, sent bounty hunters after Han Solo.

Dalmatian Press

SPELL-A-VICEROY MAZE

Go through the maze along the path that spells "Nute" Gunray.

START

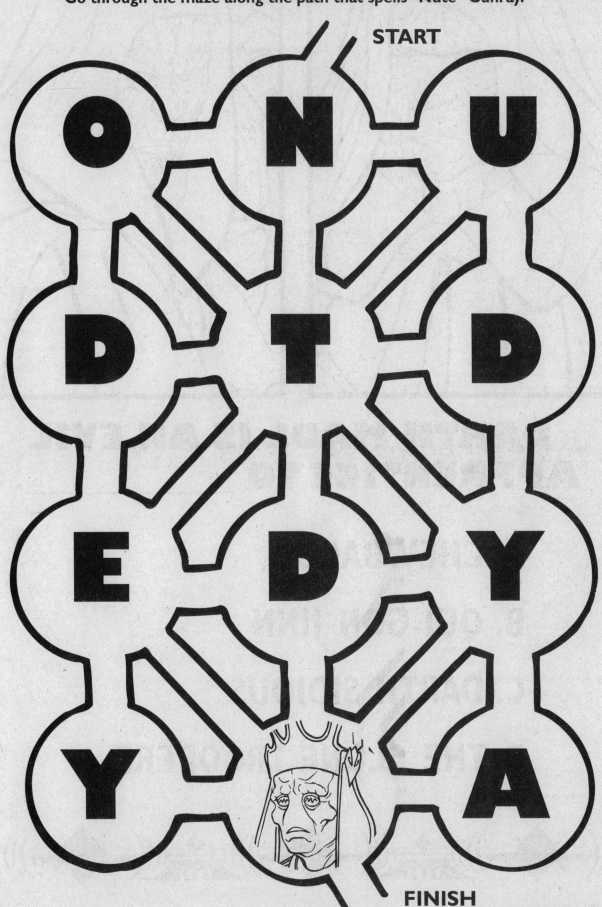

FINISH

DARTH MAUL IS AN EVIL APPRENTICE TO _____.

A. CHEWBACCA

B. QUI-GON JINN

C. DARTH SIDIOUS

D. THE CLONE TROOPERS

Dalmatian Press

"THAT'S NO MOON!"

Which square completes the drawing?

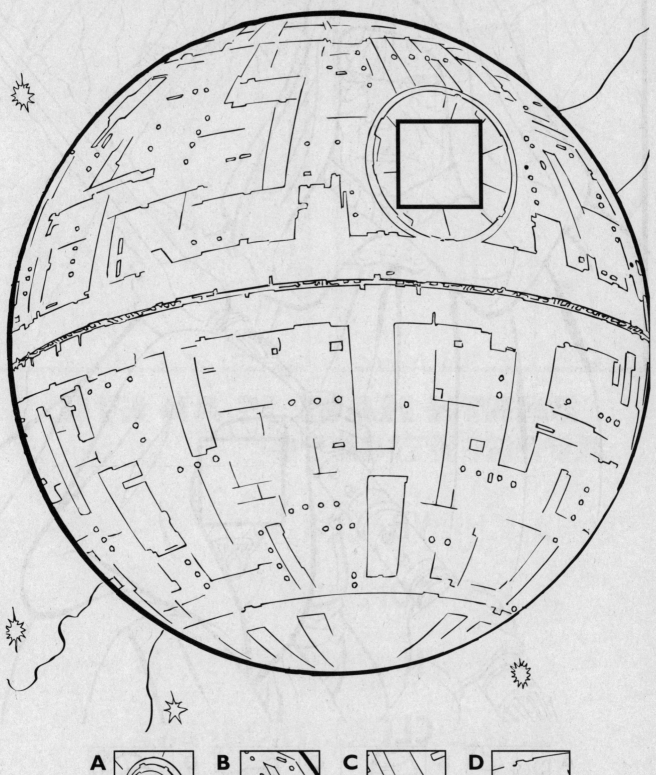

A   B   C   D

Your answer: _____

Answer: A

"...SOON WE WILL REVENGE."

Which square completes the drawing?

A   B   C   D

Your answer: _____

DARTH MAUL'S CROSSWORD PUZZLE

Down:
1. Darth Maul's ship, a Sith _____.
2. The color of Darth Maul's robes.

Across:
3. A Sith, Darth Maul's Master, Darth _____.
4. Darth Maul's _____ has two blades.
5. They are this color.
6. They stick out of the top of Darth Maul's head, giving him a frightening appearance.

Answers: 1. Infiltrator, 2. black, 3. Sidious, 4. lightsaber, 5. red, 6. horns

SITH
APPRENTICE

With a friend, take turns connecting the dots with a single straight line, up and down or left and right. When the connected lines complete a box, color that box with your color. When all the dots are connected and all the completed boxes colored, count the colored boxes. The warrior with the most colored boxes will become a Sith apprentice using the dark side of the Force.

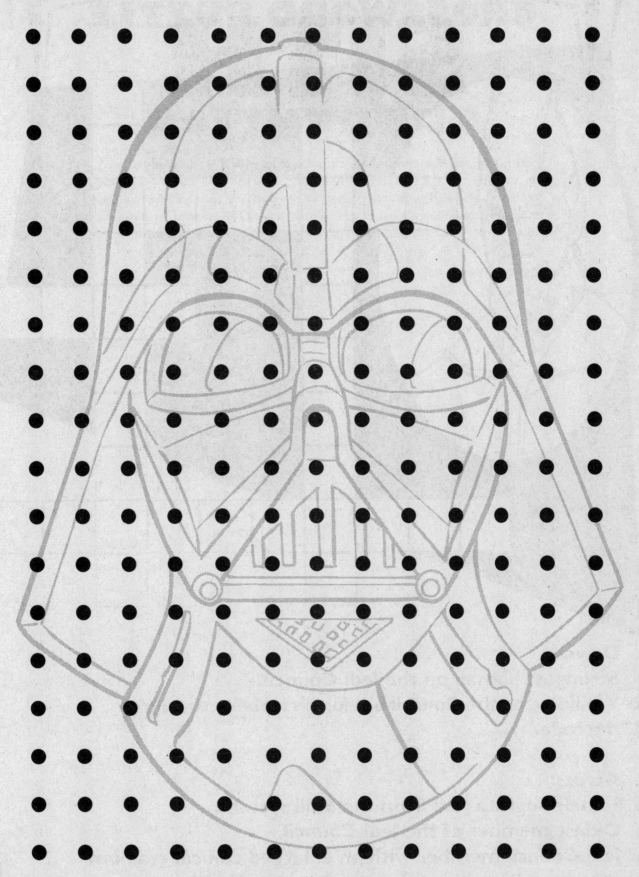

JEDI COUNCIL CROSSWORD PUZZLE

Down:

1. Strongest human on the Jedi Council.
2. Would be on the Council but for his inability to follow the code.

Across:

3. Female Togruta Jedi from the Shili system.
4. Oldest member of the Jedi Council.
5. Jedi Council member with an enlarged conical cranium that contains a binary brain (pictured above).

Dalmatian Press

WHO IS NOT ON THE JEDI COUNCIL?

A. QUI-GON JINN

B. MACE WINDU

C. YODA

D. KI-ADI-MUNDI

Answer: A

WHICH SHIP MADE THE KESSEL RUN THE FASTEST?

A. *THE MILLENNIUM FALCON*

B. FEDERATION DROID FIGHTERS

C. J-TYPE 327, NUBIAN VESSEL

D. AN X-WING FIGHTER

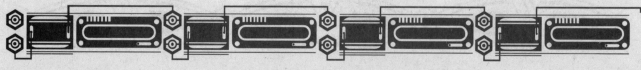

Dalmatian Press

WHO IS THE PHANTOM MENACE?

A. DARTH BANE

B. DARTH MAUL

C. DARTH VADER

D. DARTH SIDIOUS

PODRACE WORD SEARCH

Look forwards, backwards, across, down and diagonally to find the names listed below:

Anakin   Sebulba   Tatooine
Boonta Eve   Fode   Beed
Ody   Gasgano   Mos Espa

POD - RACE

M	A	B	O	O	N	T	A	E
O	D	Y	P	C	Q	D	N	V
S	R	B	X	I	J	I	A	E
E	H	E	T	F	O	E	K	D
S	Y	E	Z	O	F	V	I	O
P	N	D	T	U	O	W	N	F
A	G	A	S	G	A	N	O	R
Z	T	A	B	L	U	B	E	S
K	T	S	E	L	G	M	B	S

WHO IS THE TWO-HEADED COMMENTATOR FOR THE PODRACE?

A. LUKE & LEIA

B. HAN & CHEWBACCA

C. OBI-WAN & QUI-GON

D. FODE & BEED

Answer: D

WHO DOESN'T BELONG?

Who is not from Naboo?

A

B

C

D

Your answer: _____

Dalmatian Press

JEDI ORDER WORD SEARCH

Look forwards, backwards, across, down and diagonally to find the words listed below:

Coruscant   Temple   Master
Jedi   Padawan   Yoda
Obi-Wan   Qui-Gon   Knight
Yaddle   Mace Windu   Anakin

T	E	M	P	L	E	A	E	M
N	A	W	A	D	A	P	L	A
A	N	A	K	I	N	C	D	C
C	M	J	D	F	N	K	D	E
S	A	H	E	G	A	N	A	W
U	S	K	L	D	W	I	Y	I
R	T	Z	Q	U	I	G	O	N
O	E	T	Y	I	B	H	D	D
C	R	B	J	E	O	T	A	U

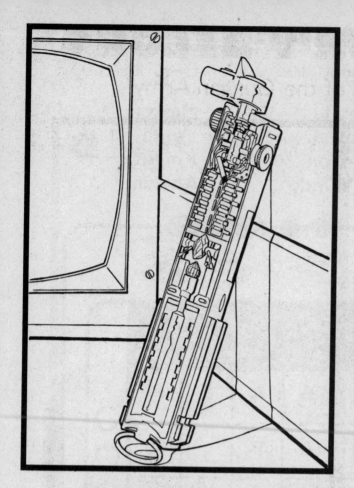

WHAT IS THE PREFERRED WEAPON OF THE JEDI?

A. POINTED STICKS

B. A BLASTER RIFLE

C. KAMINOAN POISON DART

D. LIGHTSABER

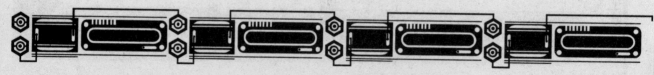

Dalmatian Press

WHAT DOESN'T BELONG?

Which is not a part of the Gungan Army?

A

B

C

D

Your answer: _____

WHO DOESN'T BELONG?

Who doesn't live on Tatooine?

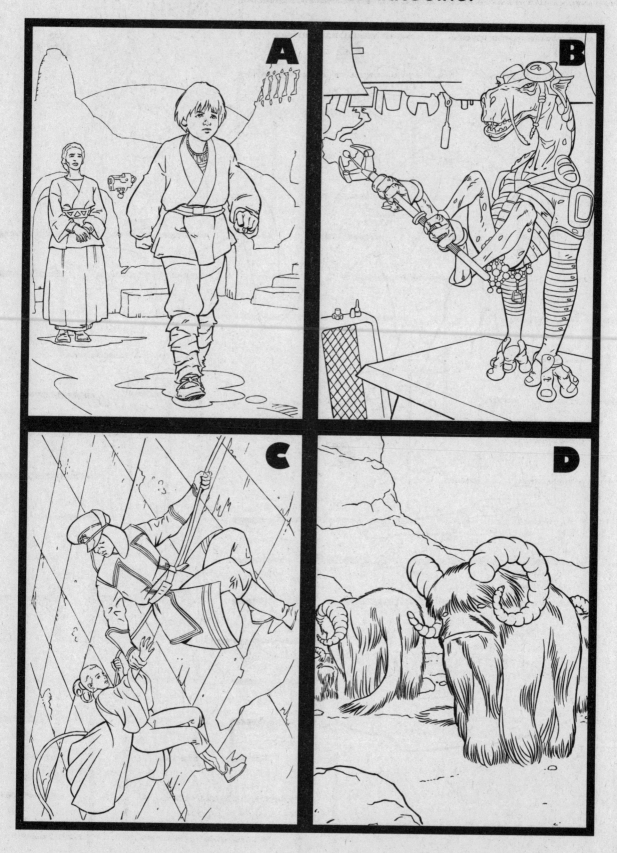

Your answer: _____

SETTLING THE TRADE BLOCKADE

Guide the Republic Cruiser through the maze and settle the dispute with the Neimoidians.

FINISH

START

© Lucasfilm Ltd.

WHO DOESN'T BELONG?

Who is not a member of the Skywalker family?

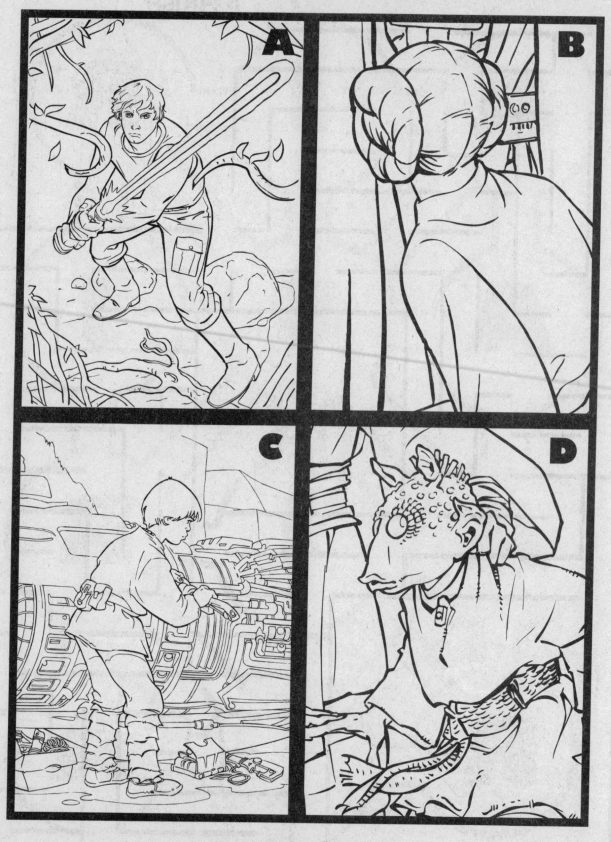

Your answer:_____

Dalmatian Press

SPELL-A-GUNGAN MAZE

Go through the maze along the path that spells "Jar Jar."

START

FINISH

TO WHOM DOES WATTO OWE CREDITS AFTER LOSING A BET?

A. JANGO FETT

B. JABBA THE HUTT

C. DARTH VADER

D. EMPEROR PALPATINE

Dalmatian Press

WHO DOESN'T BELONG?

Which scene doesn't involve Qui-Gon Jinn?

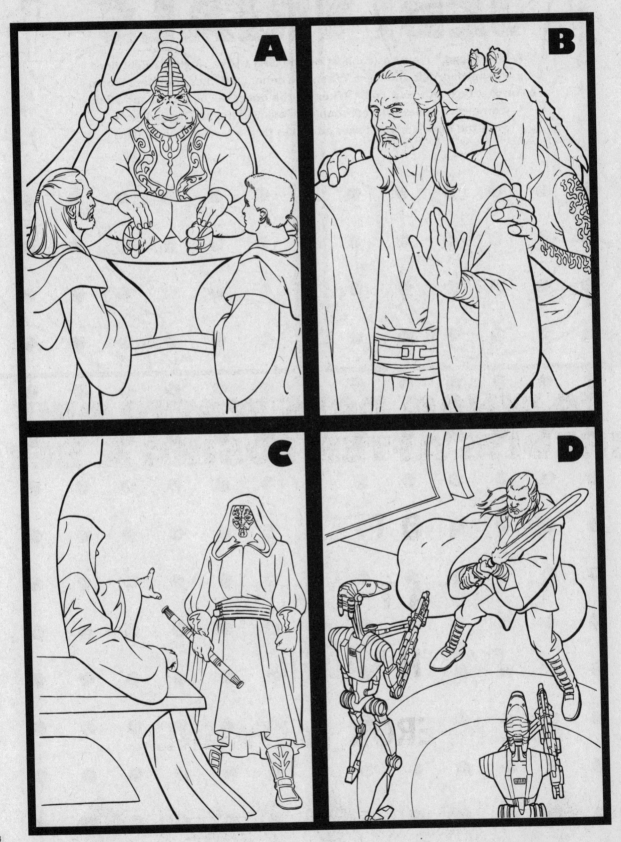

Your answer: _____

Answer: C

JEDI TRIALS

With a friend, take turns connecting the dots with a single straight line, up and down or left and right. When the connected lines complete a box, color that box with your color. When all the dots are connected and all the completed boxes colored, count the colored boxes. The Padawan with the most colored boxes advances to the level of Jedi Knight.

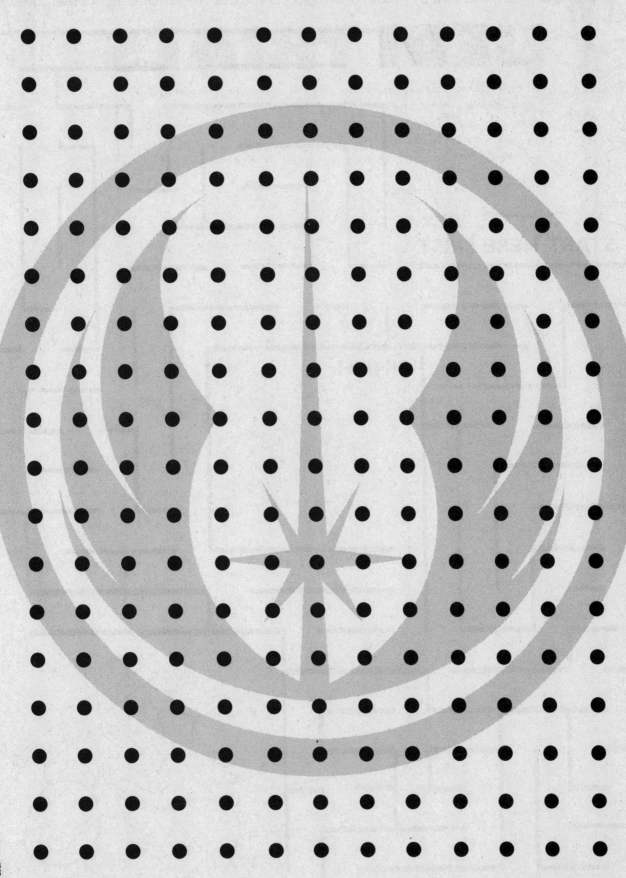

DUEL OF THE FATES

Lead Qui-Gon and Darth Maul to the center of the maze for a lightsaber duel.

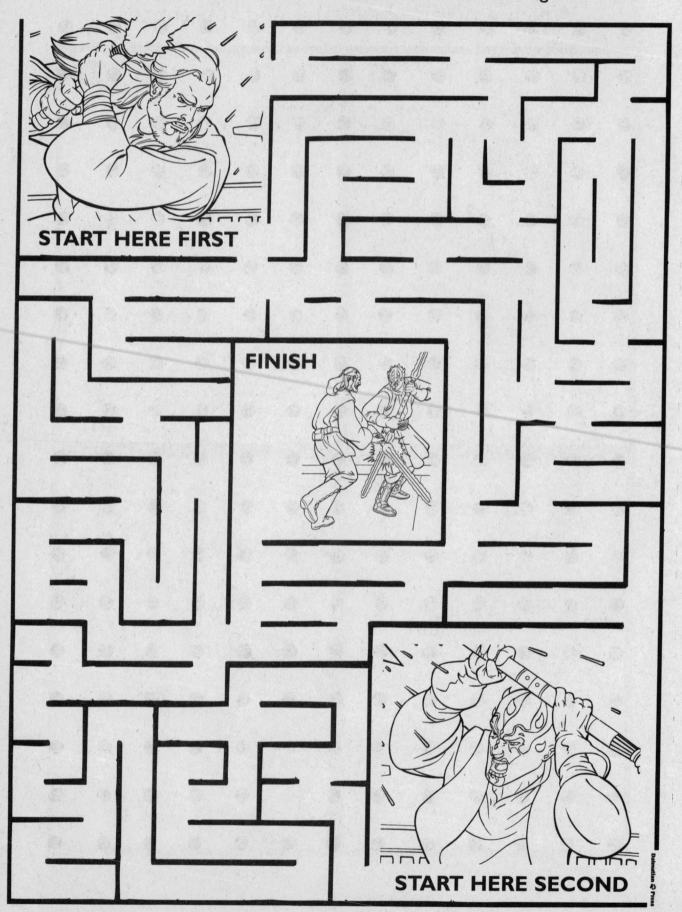

START HERE FIRST

FINISH

START HERE SECOND

WHO DOESN'T BELONG?

Which group is not Master and apprentice?

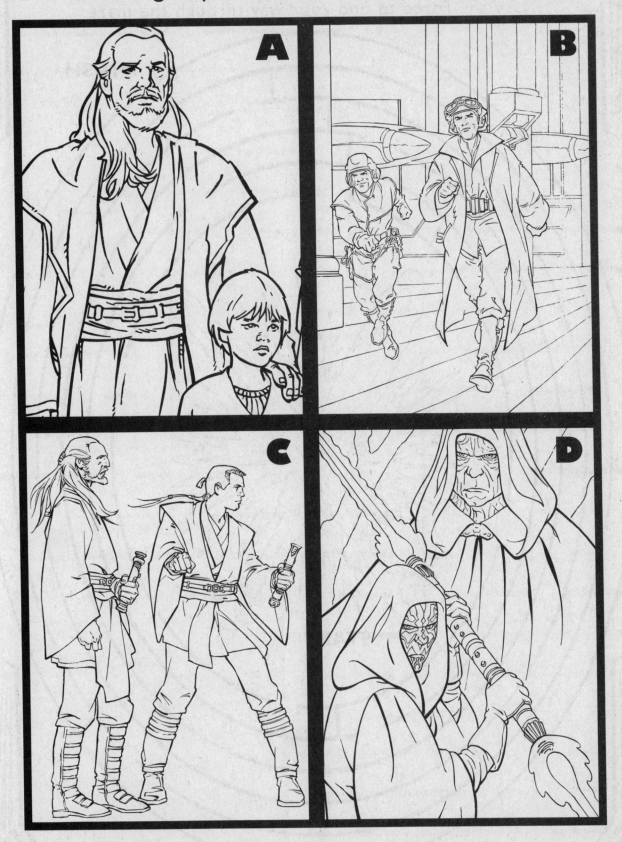

Your answer: _____

Answer: B

LIGHTSABER DUEL

Use the Force to find your way through the maze.

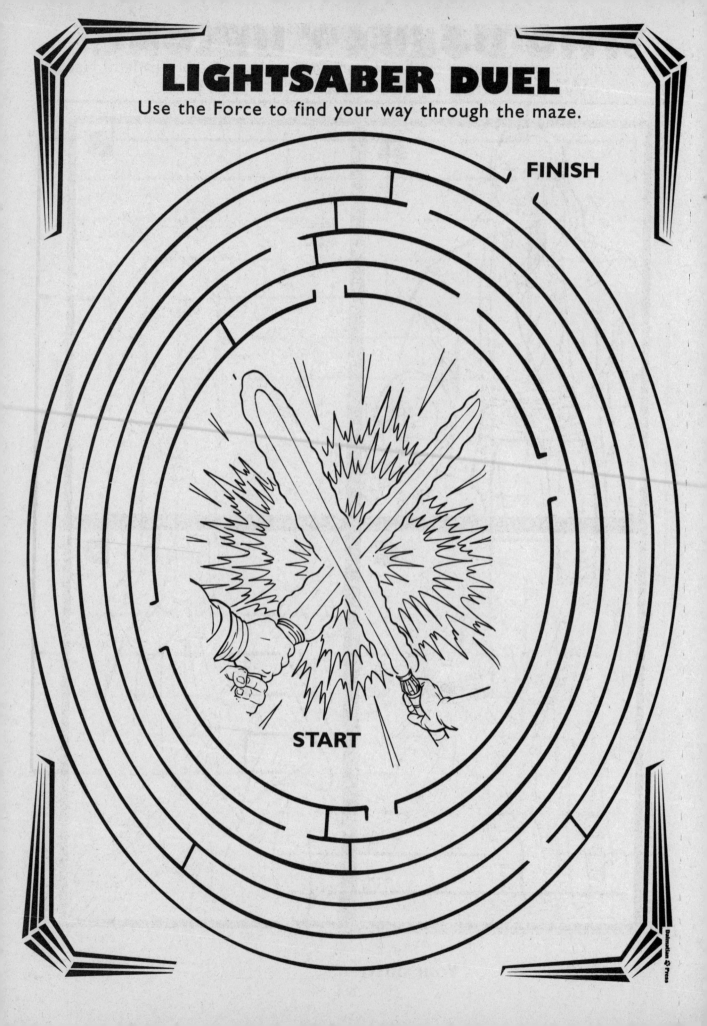

FINISH

START

HOSTILE NEGOTIATIONS

Lead the Jedi through the maze to the Neimoidians, and end the blockade of Naboo.

START

FINISH

TIGHT FORMATION

Guide the lost starfighter through the maze and back to his squadron.

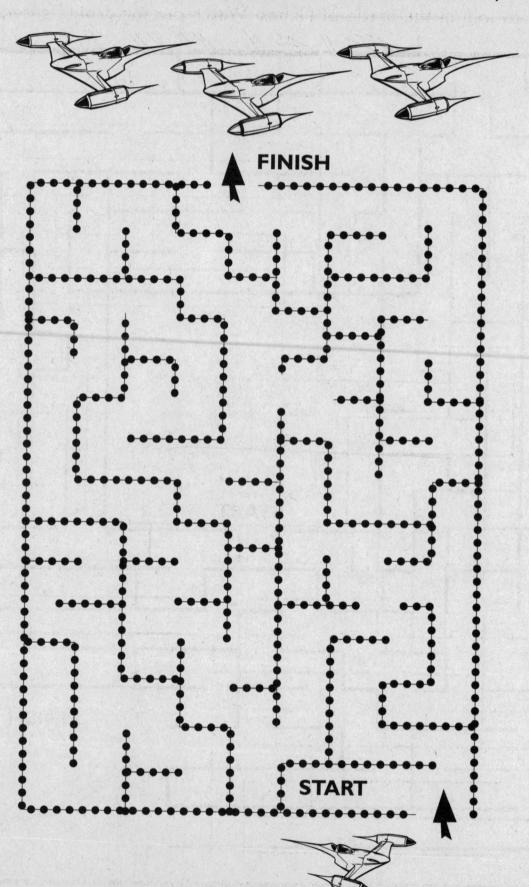

FINISH

START

ACCIDENTAL HERO

Help Anakin find his way to the Trade Federation Battleship to join in the battle of Naboo. Watch out for droid fighters.

START

FINISH

© Lucasfilm Ltd.

THIRSTY AMBASSADORS

Help TC-14 bring refreshments to the Ambassadors
of the Supreme Chancellor, but watch out for battle droids.

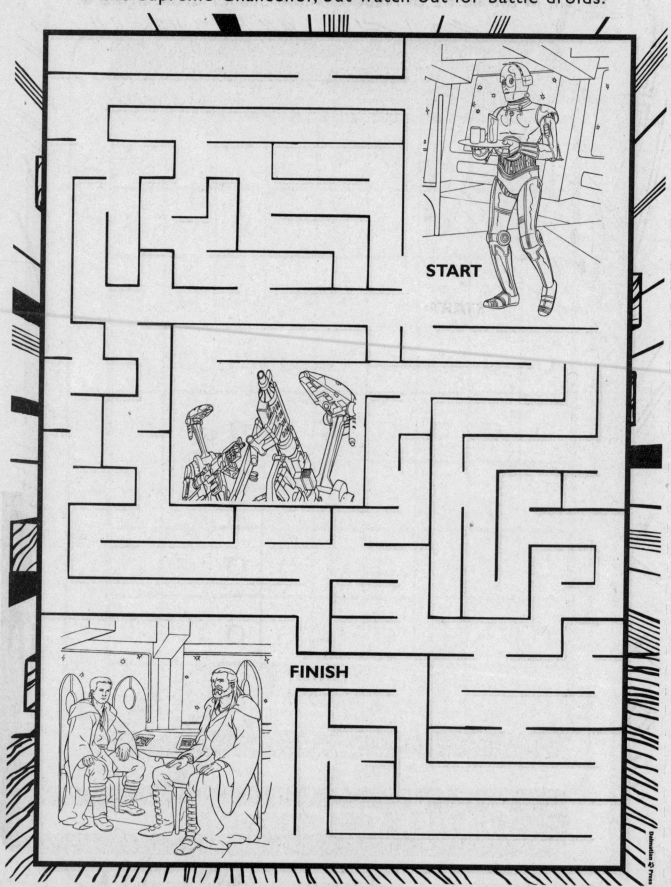

START

FINISH

MIDI-CHLORIAN COUNT

Your Answer:

_____

Using this Jedi communicator, count how many midi-chlorians Qui-Gon found in Anakin's blood.

	σ	σ	σ	σ	σ	σ		σ
σ	σ	σ	σ	σ	σ	σ	σ	σ
σ	σ	σ		σ	σ	σ	σ	σ
σ	σ	σ	σ	σ	σ	σ	σ	σ
σ	σ	σ	σ	σ		σ	σ	σ
σ	σ	σ	σ	σ	σ	σ	σ	σ
σ	σ	σ	σ	σ	σ	σ	σ	σ
σ		σ	σ	σ	σ		σ	
σ	σ	σ	σ	σ		σ	σ	σ

THE MIGHTY JABBA THE HUTT

Help Jabba throw his prisoners to the hungry Sarlacc.

START

FINISH

Dalmatian Press

WHO DOESN'T BELONG?

Which is not a Jedi group?

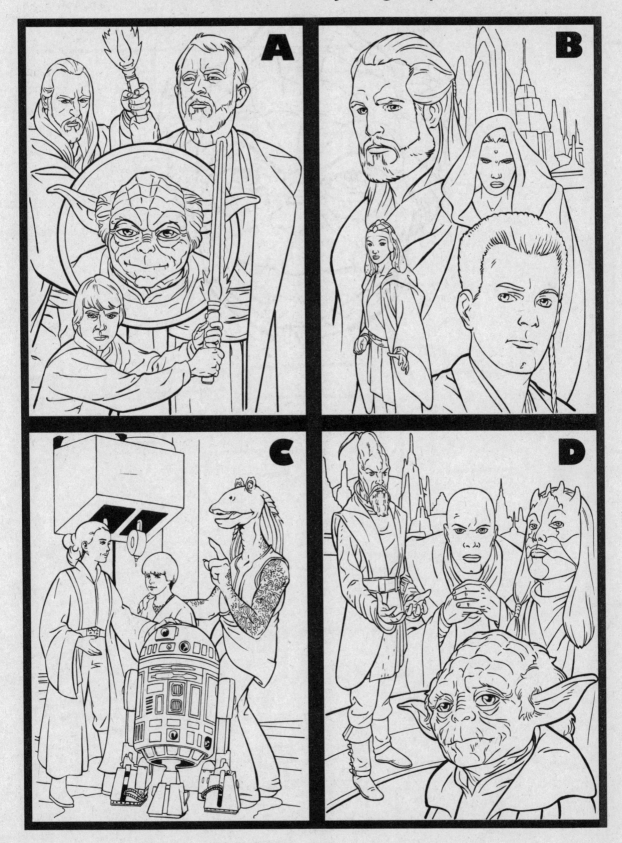

Your answer: _____

Answer: C

"HEAR YOU, I CANNOT."
Draw the parts of Master Yoda's body that are missing.

YODA'S SURPRISE

Wind your way through the grid to spell out the surprise Yoda has under his cloak for anyone who underestimates his power as a Jedi Master. Start with the circled "G."

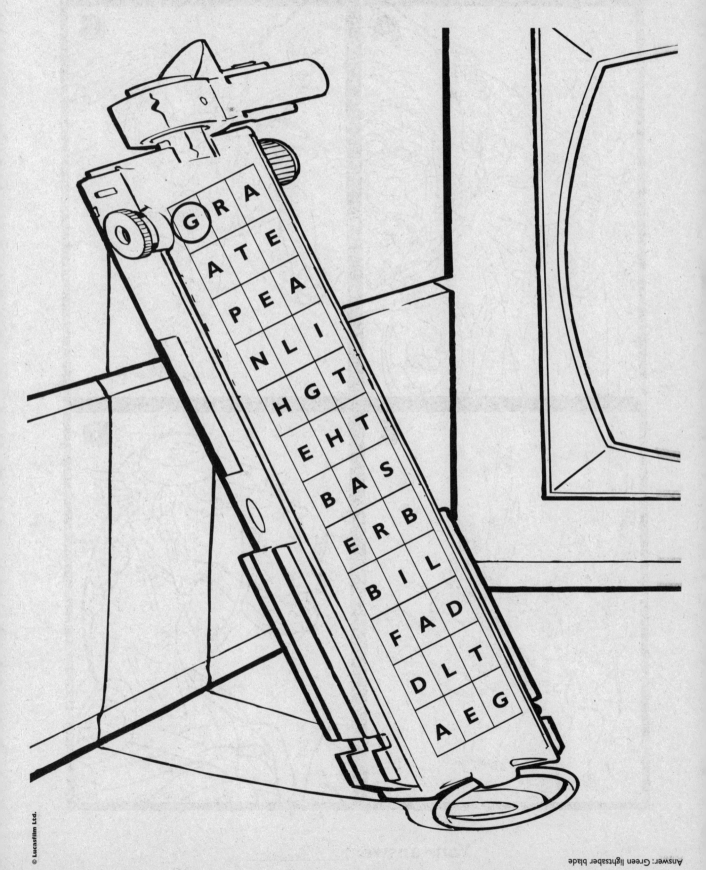

WHO DOESN'T BELONG?

Who is not a Gungan?

Your answer: _____

CORUSCANT MAZE

The entire planet is one big city. Find your way from one side to the other.

START

FINISH

FOR WHOM DOES ANAKIN PILOT HIS PODRACER?

A. JABBA THE HUTT

B. MACE WINDU

C. WATTO

D. JANGO FETT

Dalmatian Press

WHAT DOESN'T BELONG?

Which one doesn't travel through space?

Your answer: _____

Answer: B

BECOME A JEDI KNIGHT!

Draw yourself in Jedi robes.

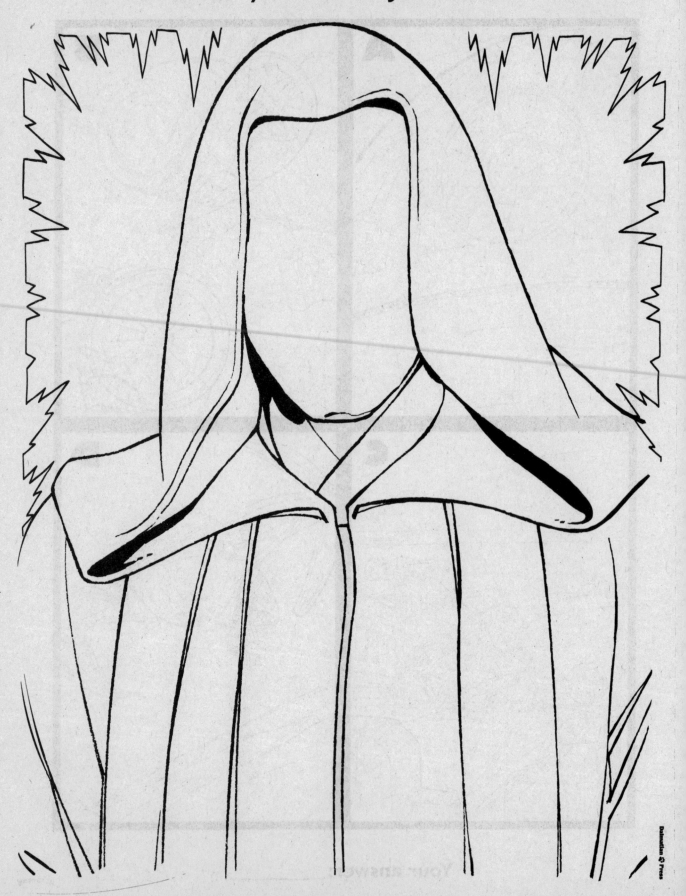

WHAT DOESN'T BELONG?

Which one is not a droid?

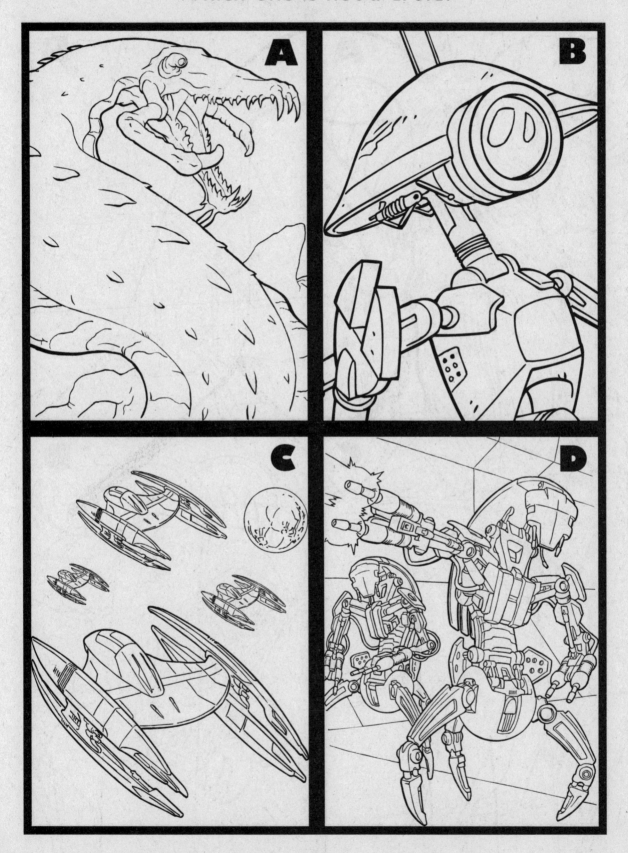

Your answer: _____

Answer: A

WHAT DOESN'T BELONG?

Which one is not an animal?

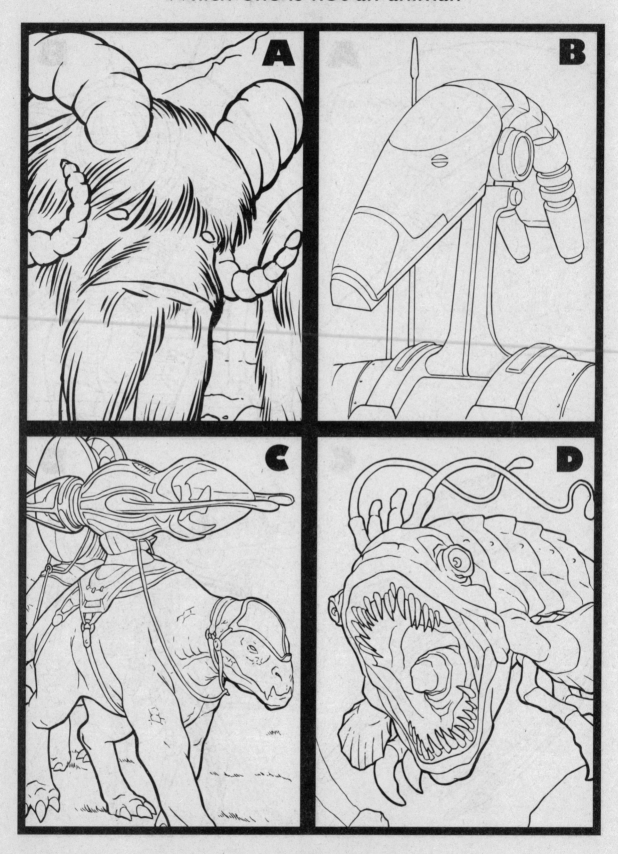

Your answer: _____

WHAT DOESN'T BELONG?

Which one is not a pit droid?

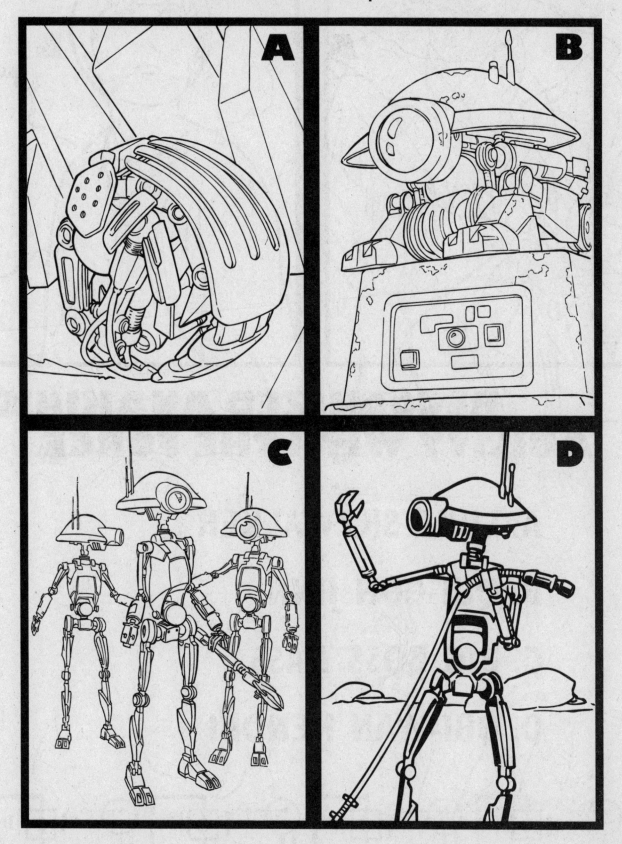

Your answer: _____

_____ RECOGNIZED ANAKIN'S ABILITY WITH THE FORCE.

A. LUKE SKYWALKER

B. QUI-GON JINN

C. BIG BOSS NASS

D. OBI-WAN KENOBI

Dalmatian Press

WHO DOESN'T BELONG?

Who is not a Sith?

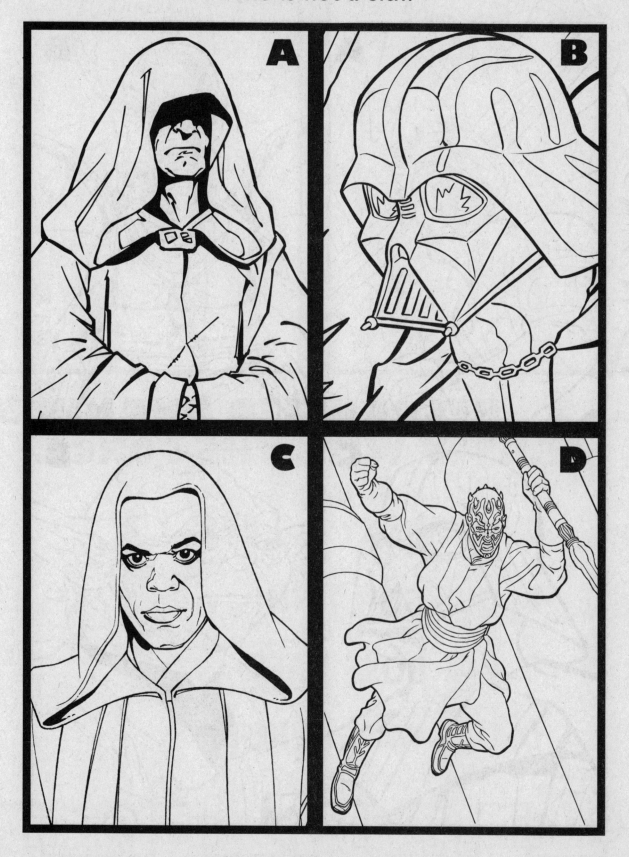

Your answer: _____

Answer: C

WHO DOESN'T BELONG?

Who was never a Jedi?

Your answer: _____

RULE THE UNIVERSE!

Draw yourself as a Sith who uses the dark side of the Force.

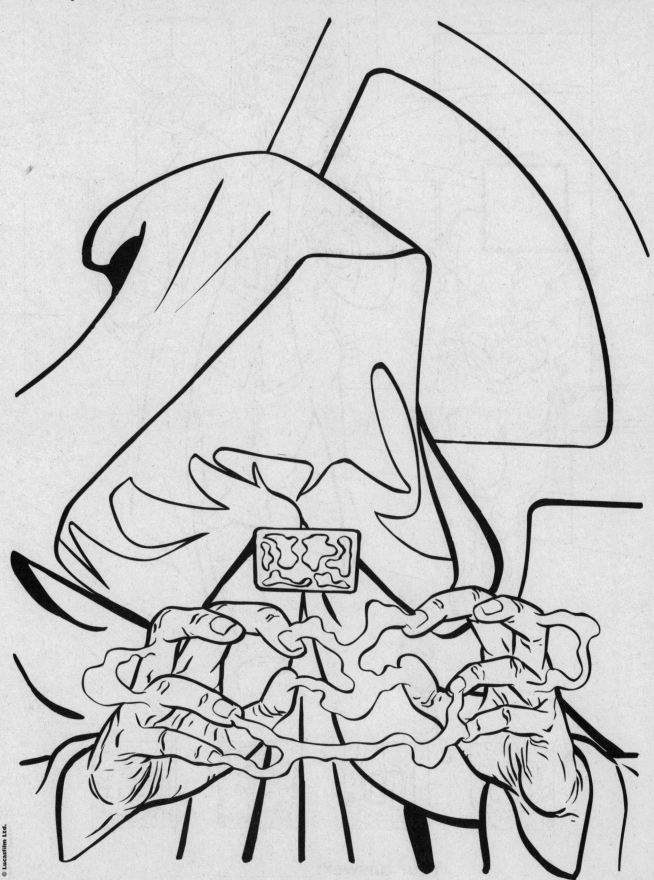

TO THE FIGHTERS

Which square completes the drawing?

A   B   C   D

Your answer: _____

WHO DOESN'T BELONG?

Who didn't race in the Boonta Eve Podrace?

Your answer: _____

Answer: D

WHAT DOESN'T BELONG?

Which one is not a battle droid?

Your answer: _____

Dalmatian Press

Anger is not the way of the Jedi.

JEDI VS. SITH

With a friend, take turns connecting the dots with a single straight line,
up and down or right and left. When the connected lines complete a box,
color that box with your color. When all the dots are connected
and all the completed boxes colored, count the colored boxes.
The player with the most colored boxes wins the duel.

WHO WINS THE BOONTA EVE PODRACE?

A. BEN QUADINAROS

B. A PIT DROID

C. SEBULBA

D. ANAKIN SKYWALKER

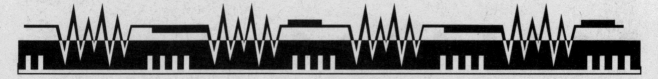

THROUGH THE PLANET'S CORE

Guide the bongo with Jar Jar, Qui-Gon and Obi-Wan through the planet's core.

START

FINISH

BUILD-A-BOT

The Destroyer droid is not finished.
Draw a line to the part that completes him.

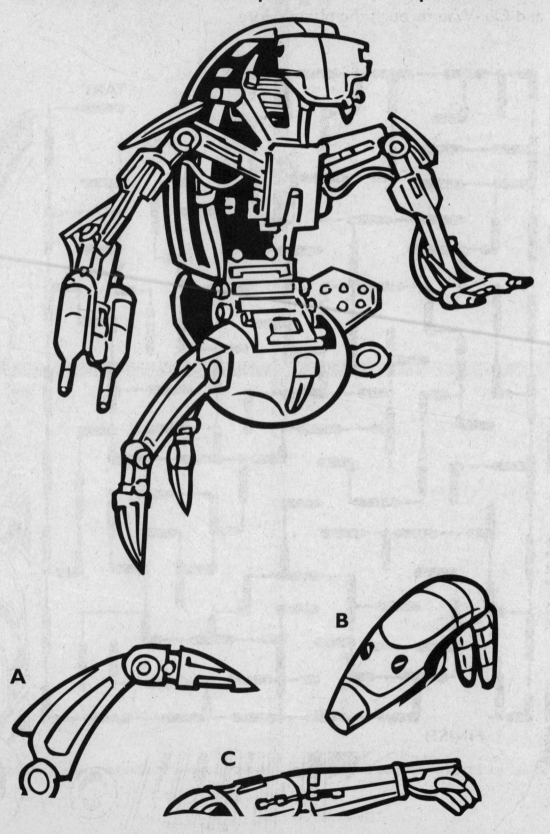

A

B

C

WHAT DOESN'T BELONG?

Which one is not a Destroyer droid?

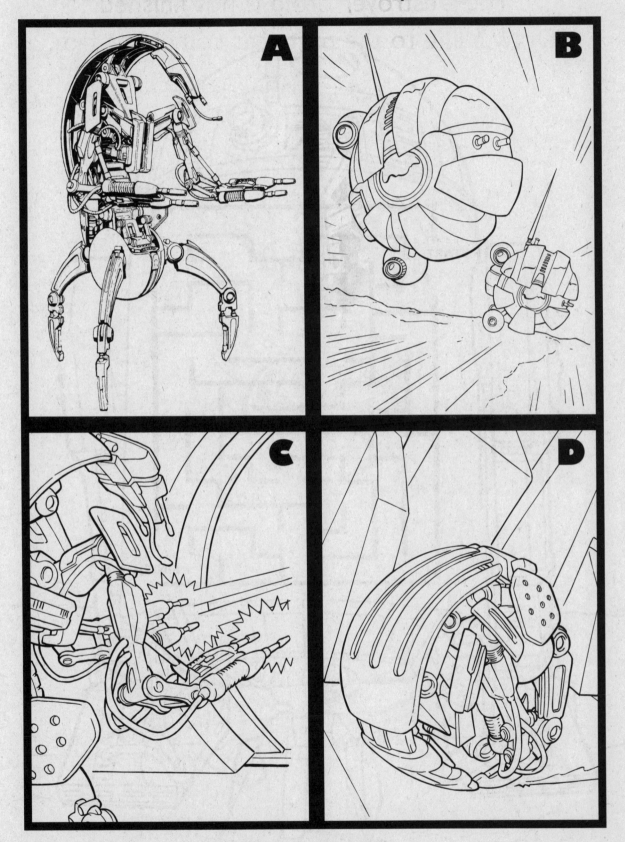

Your answer: _____

Answer: B

INSIDE R2-D2

Droids are very complicated inside. Find your way through R2-D2.

START

FINISH

CORUSCANT LANDING

Navigate a safe landing for Senator Amidala through the busy skyways of Coruscant.

START

FINISH

THE BATTLE OF YAVIN 4

With a friend, take turns connecting the dots with a single straight line,
up and down or left and right. When the connected lines complete a box,
color that box with your color. When all the dots are connected
and all the completed boxes colored, count the colored boxes.
The player with the most colored boxes wins the "Battle of Yavin 4."

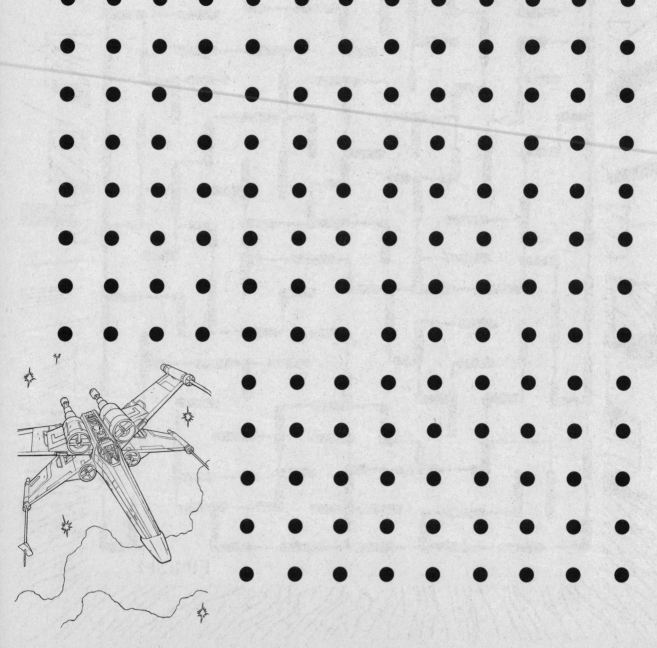

IN THE PODRACES, ON WHOM DOES EVERYONE BET?

A. BEN QUADINAROS

B. QUI-GON JINN

C. SEBULBA

D. ANAKIN SKYWALKER

Dalmatian Press

DESIGN-A-DROID

How would you draw the bottom half of this pit droid?

HOORAY FOR THE HEROES

Which square completes the drawing?

 **A**   **B**   **C**  **D**

Your answer: _____

CELEBRATING A VICTORY

Which square completes the drawing?

A  B C D

Your answer: _____

Answer: D

BUILD-A-BOT

C-3PO is not finished.
Draw a line to the part
that completes him.

A

B

C

D

Answer: D

DESTROY THE DEATH STAR

Use the Force to guide Luke's proton torpedoes down
the thermal exhaust shaft and destroy the Death Star.

START

FINISH

IN THE BATTLE OF NABOO, CAPTAIN _____ FOUGHT AGAINST THE BATTLE DROIDS.

A. TARPALS

B. JAR JAR

C. CHEWBACCA

D. HAN SOLO

Dalmatian Press

FINISH DRAWING THE REST OF BOSS NASS' FACE.

THE BATTLE OF NABOO

With a friend, take turns connecting the dots with a single straight line,
up and down or left and right. When the connected lines complete a box,
color that box with your color. When all the dots are connected
and all the completed boxes colored, count the colored boxes.
The player with the most colored boxes wins the "Battle of Naboo."

A NEW HOPE
CROSSWORD PUZZLE

Down:

1. Family name of Luke and his father.
2. The Death _____ was destroyed at the battle of Yavin.

Across:

3. Instructed Luke in the ancient ways of the Jedi, and lived on the Dagobah system.
4. Luke lost his right _____ in a duel with Darth Vader.
5. The Force flows through a _____.

Dalmatian Press

USE THE FORCE, LUKE.

Which square completes the drawing?

A   B   C   D

Your answer: _____

THE EMPEROR AND DARTH VADER USE WHAT SIDE OF THE FORCE?

A. THE LEFT SIDE

B. THE SUNNY SIDE

C. THE DARK SIDE

D. THE BRIGHT SIDE

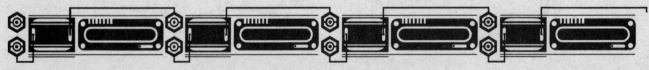

Dalmatian Press

WHERE IS THE REBEL BASE?

Which square completes the drawing?

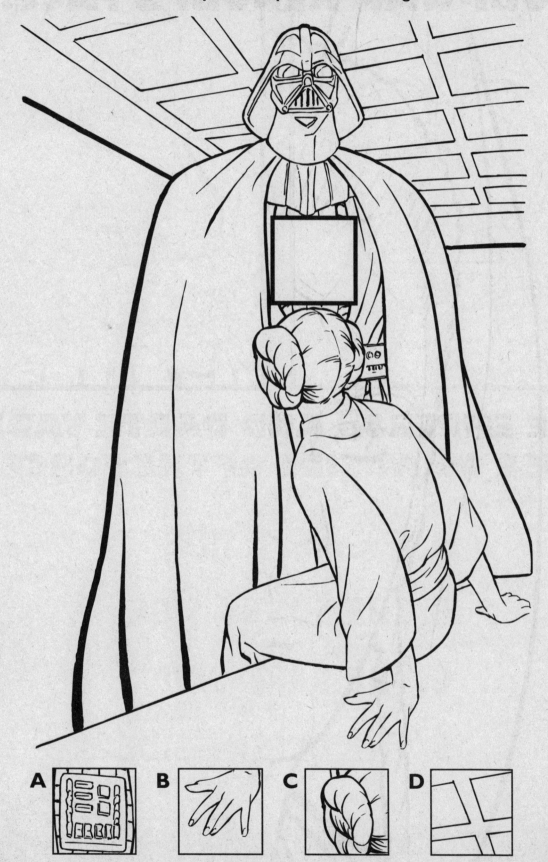

A   B   C   D

Your answer: _____

Answer: A

DRAW THE OTHER HALF OF OBI-WAN KENOBI'S FACE.

ANAKIN SKYWALKER'S CROSSWORD PUZZLE

Down:

1. Anakin won the Boonta Eve _____.
2. Jedi Master and first mentor to Anakin.

Across:

3. Protocol droid constucted by young Anakin.
4. Astromech droid in Anakin's fighter during the battle of Naboo.
5. Owner of young Anakin.
6. Anakin was freed from being a _____ after Qui-Gon won his bet with Watto.

Answers: 1. Podrace, 2. Qui-Gon, 3. C-3PO, 4. R2-D2, 5. Watto, 6. slave.

THE FORCE WILL BE WITH YOU... ALWAYS.

Which square completes the drawing?

A 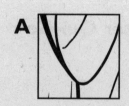 B  C 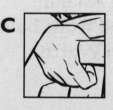 D

Your answer: _____

Dalmatian Press